COMPLETE GUIDE TO FISHING

Spinning & Baitcasting

COMPLETE GUIDE TO FISHING
Spinning & Baitcasting

MASON CREST PUBLISHERS, INC.

COMPLETE GUIDE TO FISHING – **Spinning & Baitcasting**
has been originated, produced and designed by AB Nordbok,
Gothenburg, Sweden.

Publisher
Gunnar Stenmar

Editorial chief
Anders Walberg

Design, setting & photowork:
Reproman AB, Gothenburg, Sweden

Translator:
Jon van Leuven

Nordbok would like to express sincere thanks to all
persons and companies who have contributed in
different ways to the production of this book.

World copyright © 2002
Nordbok International,
P.O.Box 7095
SE-402 32 Gothenburg, Sweden.

Published in the United States by
Mason Crest Publishers, Inc.
370 Reed Road, Broomall, PA 19008
(866) MCP-BOOK (toll free)
www.masoncrest.com

First printing
1 2 3 4 5 6 7 8 9 10
Library of Congress Cataloging-in-Publication Data on file at
the Library of Congress

ISBN 1-59084-493-9

Printed and bound in Jordan 2002

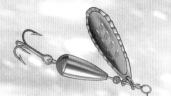

Contents

Preface

Millions of sportfishermen around the world devote themselves every day to spinning and baitcasting. Its enormous popularity reflects the fact that most well-liked species of fish can be challenged and caught in this way, but also the virtually unlimited variations that are offered by this form of sportfishing.

Fishing with artificial and natural baits is both simple and effective. These are among the main reasons why beginners and experienced fishermen tend to agree that spinning and baitcasting is the best choice of method when fishing for many species in either fresh or marine waters.

The hallmark of spinning and baitcasting is that you cast out the bait. This is true regardless of whether you fish with spoons, plugs, small spinners, or natural baits on tackle that are presented with sinkers, floats and different types of casting weights.

Another feature of this kind of fishing is that it focuses almost entirely on predatory fish: species which, during certain periods, are active hunters, primarily of smaller fish. Therefore the baits, by their form, movement, colour, smell, sound, consistency, and even taste, should be as naturalistic as possible in imitating the fish's prey – and attracting it to bite.

The equipment, baits, and fishing methods for pursuing effective spinning and baitcasting are constantly being improved and refined today, with adaptation to different fishing waters, species, and techniques.

Equipment

No equipment is so all-round that it suffices for everything from trout and salmon to pike and bass – or for fishing in both big and small waters. One can, though, require that the gear be adapted to as many forms of spinning and baitcasting as possible. If different kinds of fishing are envisaged, several setups are therefore necessary: for example, a light one-handed rod for small waters, a light two-handed rod for larger fish and waters, and a stronger two-handed rod for heavy spinning.

Lacking the right rod and a suitable reel with correct line strength, casts that are far and exact enough cannot be made. In addition, the rod and reel must be able to guide the bait's movements while retrieving it, and to register the faintest take.

Hardly a year goes by without the tackle manufacturers announcing new refinements and clever details on rods and reels that are to render them indispensable. The really essential point is thus to evaluate one's needs, not just rely on printed advice. Indeed, those with most experience in spinning and baitcasting have learned to limit their equipment.

Rods

The development of rods has gone forward much faster than that of reels. Fibreglass rods predominated during the 1960s, and carbon-fibre rods arrived in the early 1970s. The latter were at first considered too expensive for widespread acceptance, but some years later came cheap composite rods – with a blend of fibreglass and graphite, which is now most common.

Graphite and composite rods have many advantages over the earlier fibreglass rods. They are lighter, relax faster after the cast, are more obedient when retrieving, and can better register cautious takes as well as the movements of artificial lures.

Action and length

A rod's action, or how it responds when casting and playing out a fish, is determined partly by the thickness of the rod and partly by how the material is used.

Slow action describes a rod that bends along its entire length. It casts accurately, has the backbone to wear out a fish and the resilience to withstand dives. Unfortunately, they are often not strong enough to set the hook well and they require an experienced angler.

A medium-action rod has more power for setting the hook as well as the backbone and stiffness necessary for high casting precision. Only the tip half of the rod bends when playing the fish.

Fast-action rods bend in the upper third section. They have good casting qualities, set the hook fast and hard and have backbone, but do not cast accurately. Because the action is in the tip one-third of the rod, these rods are less sensitive during retrieval.

Extra fast action means that only the top one-quarter of the rod bends. This type of rod has fantastic casting abilities and is often used for competition casting and surf casting, but this means that little action is transferred down the rod to the hand grip. For surf casting using natural bait, a slow-action rod is often used instead.

It should be remembered that the rod action does not indicate what casting weight the rod is suited for.

The rod's strength and its ability to cast various weights are determined by the tapering of the tip and the diameter of the rod as well as the mixture and use of the component materials. Throughout the years manufacturers have used several simple but effective systems to choose the right rod. Some designate the casting weight, such as 14-28 grams (1/2-1 oz) which means that the rod is strong enough to cast lures of that weight. As a rule, lures weighing 8-10 grams (1/4-3/8 oz) and as much as 35 grams .(11/4 oz) can be cast on such a rod. But the casting weight limits cannot be stretched too far. Other manufacturers use a number system, often dividing rods into fourweight classes. For example, class 1 would include ultra-light rods with casting weights of 2-10 grams (1/16-3/8 oz). Class 2 weights are 10-20 grams (3/8-3/4 oz), class 3 are 20-30 grams (3/4-11/8 oz), and class 4 includes casting weights of 40-100 grams (1 1/2-3 1/2 oz). The classes give no information about the length of a rod.

Some fishing situations call for particular rod lengths and for that reason it is a good idea to follow a few general rules when choosing a rod. Boat fishing often needs a shorter rod

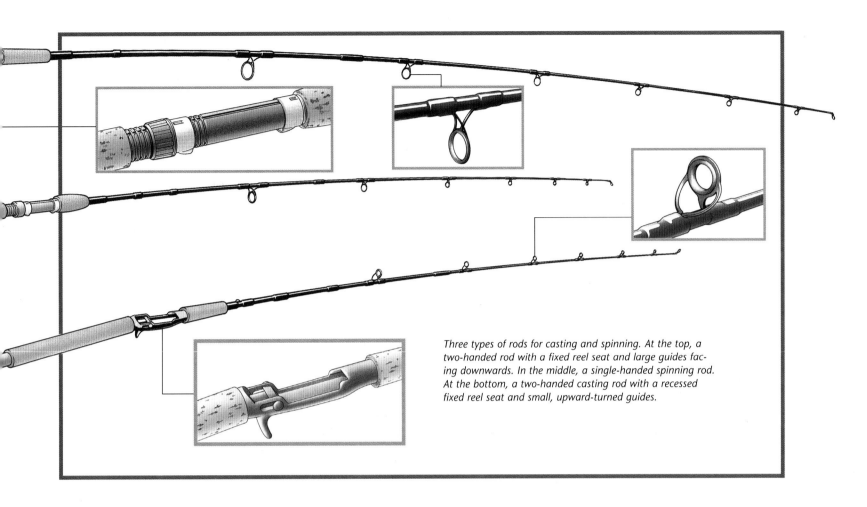

Three types of rods for casting and spinning. At the top, a two-handed rod with a fixed reel seat and large guides facing downwards. In the middle, a single-handed spinning rod. At the bottom, a two-handed casting rod with a recessed fixed reel seat and small, upward-turned guides.

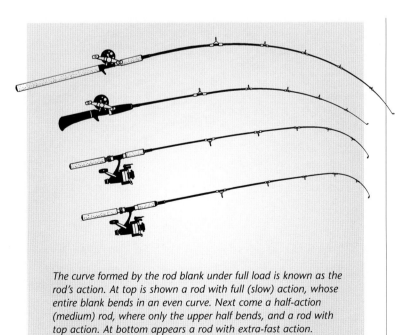

The curve formed by the rod blank under full load is known as the rod's action. At top is shown a rod with full (slow) action, whose entire blank bends in an even curve. Next come a half-action (medium) rod, where only the upper half bends, and a rod with top action. At bottom appears a rod with extra-fast action.

for light lures and slightly longer rods for heavier lures. Fishing in a small river or stream is often best with a longer rod so the lure can be kept free of trees, bushes and grass along the shore, and to provide better control of the lure in the current.

Large open water areas require a longer cast and with it a longer rod. In general, a long rod casts better than a short one, even if both are designed for the same casting weight. Long rods are more sensitive to sudden movements of a fish when being landed, but when fishing under low hanging branches a long rod will only get in the way.

Casting weight

Most rods are built for a particular casting weight. To make the rod as useful and easily sold as possible, the casting weight is often stated with a wide margin. For instance, 10-40 grams are frequently recommended on a 9-foot rod. In truth, such a rod is commonly best suited to a casting weight of 15-25 grams. It can, of course, cast with weights of both 10 and 40 grams, but then does not yield a pleasing cast, and neither does it react naturally during the cast. In order to cast artificial lures of 10 or 35-40 grams, one should instead choose a rod with a casting weight of 5-20 or 30-80 grams.

Ferrules

Most rods consist of two parts, but there are some longer two-handed rods of 11 feet that have three parts. Each joint is called a ferrule, and may be designed in different ways. A topover ferrule is most common: the rod's upper half projects down over the lower half. A spigot ferrule is among the most secure: the rod blank, built in a single piece, is cut in the middle and a short, massive graphite tube is glued into the lower part. The upper part is slid down over this spigot. On many cheap rods, the top part is simply stuck into the bottom part.

Rod guides

Ceramic guides are now standard on nearly all rods. Some years ago, ceramic guides were high-quality products from makers like Fuji and Seymo – but today many rods have guides of much worse quality. Good ceramic guides cause minimal friction and last long, but "unknown" brands can be weak and break easily. Often the latter's insert falls out or cracks form in the guide.

Ceramic guides are one-legged on light rods and two-legged on strong rods. They are also frequently bigger on spinning rods than on rods intended for multiplier reels.

Rod handles and reel seats

The rod handle consists of cork or foam rubber (EVA = evaporin). Both types are excellent and give a good grip. Most older fishermen doubtless prefer cork as a natural material, which insulates at least as well as EVA. Since many rods are standardized products, one often finds that an 8-foot rod, for example, has been provided with the same length of handle

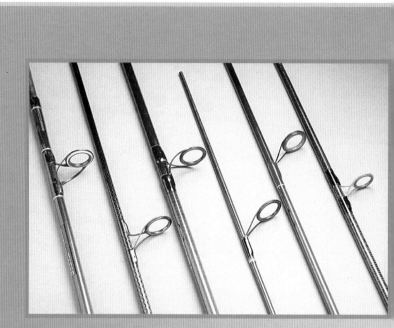

Most rods have ceramic guides. From the left are shown a standard Fuji guide, Fuji SIC guide, Seymo Supaglide, one- legged ceramic guide, one-legged guide of worse quality and (at far right) a gold-coloured rod guide of the brand Hardloy.

There are different ways of designing the joints between rod parts. Above is a top-over ferrule, the commonest joint type, with the top part slid down over the lower part. In the middle is a type of ferrule often seen on cheaper rods, with the top part slid into the lower part. Below these is a spigot ferrule, regarded as the strongest and most secure type of rod ferrule.

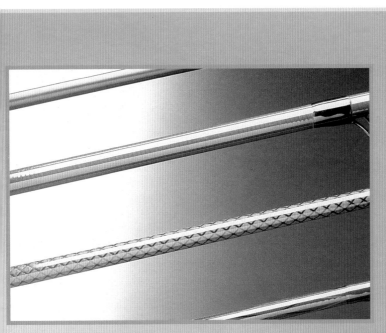

Today the majority of rods are made from graphite, but differ in the appearance and finish of their blanks. At top is a matt-polished blank of High Modulus graphite. Next come an unpolished blank and a Whisker High Modulus graphite blank. At bottom is a blank of kevlar-reinforced IM6 graphite.

Rod handles are now made almost exclusively of cork and foam (EVA-grip or a kind of foam rubber), and the reel seats primarily of composite and/or metal. In this photo are seven two-handed rods with different types of handles and reel seats. Except for multiplier rods with finger-hooks, most reel seats can be combined with both open-face spinning reels and multiplier reels.

as a 9-footer. On quality rods, however, the rod handle's bottom part is better proportioned.

The reel seat is made of metal and/or composite material, and has two locking rings. Nowadays most rods use a screw-down reel seat: the front part of the handle has a built-in threading, which locks the reel foot. It tends to be thicker than a standard handle.

On rods for multiplier reels, the seat is designed differently, even though such a reel can easily be used in ordinary seats on rods made for spinning reels. Many rods constructed for baitcasting reels have a depressed seat that allows an improved finger-grip, and commonly also a finger-hook or a pistol-grip.

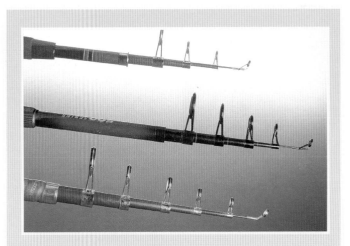

Telescopic rods

For spinning and baitcasting, telescopic rods have never been a success, apart from their great popularity in some countries like Germany. One of their disadvantages is that this construction does not give a very pleasing action. Due to the separate parts of the rod, the guides are also often too far apart, causing a lot of friction on the line – especially when playing large fish. Moreover, these rods are comparatively heavy. A telescopic rod is ideal for journeys, but the guides should always be protected by a holster during transportation.

Reels

Spinning reels and baitcasting reels are superb within their respective fields of use. A spinning reel is easiest for a beginner to operate, and it is best suited to light casting weights of 2-10 grams. A baitcasting reel, however, casts farthest with weights from 10 grams upward. This reel's structure also better conveys the feel of a fight and the contact with a fish, as the line is in direct touch with the spool during the fight. Besides, a multi-reel has very good power transmission and, therefore, makes it easier to fight big fish with a small reel.

On the other hand, in a headwind where the lures are readily blown sideways, problems can arise with a baitcasting reel: the accelerating force does not stop when the lure has been cast, and a backlash may well result. But while retrieving, the contact with the lure is better with a baitcasting reel.

Spinning reels

Anyone can learn to cast with a modern spinning reel after just a few hours' training. Sizes range from the smallest UL types, through fairly large reels that suit almost all fish species, to big reels for salmon and sea fishing. Nearly all

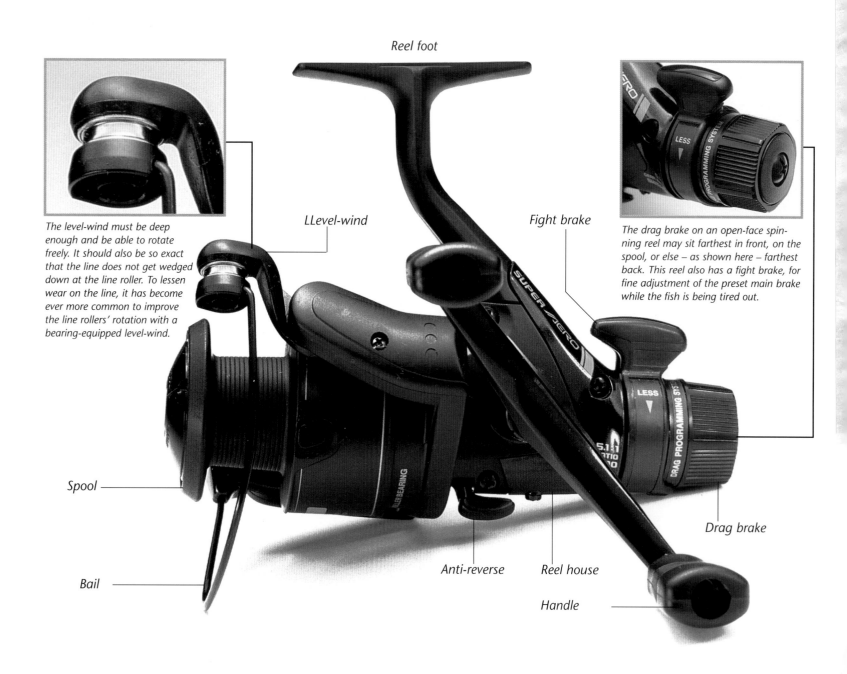

Reel foot

The level-wind must be deep enough and be able to rotate freely. It should also be so exact that the line does not get wedged down at the line roller. To lessen wear on the line, it has become ever more common to improve the line rollers' rotation with a bearing-equipped level-wind.

LLevel-wind

Fight brake

The drag brake on an open-face spinning reel may sit farthest in front, on the spool, or else – as shown here – farthest back. This reel also has a fight brake, for fine adjustment of the preset main brake while the fish is being tired out.

Spool

Bail

Anti-reverse

Reel house

Drag brake

Handle

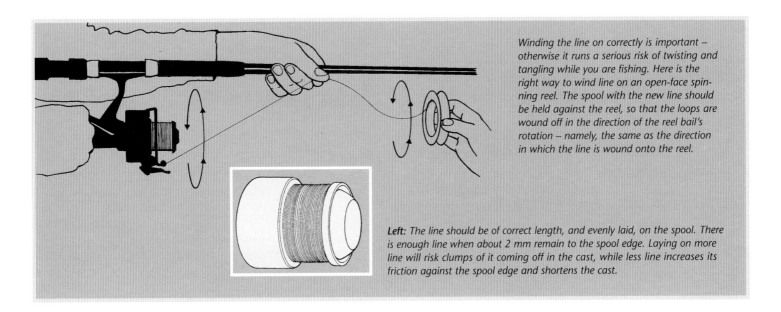

Winding the line on correctly is important – otherwise it runs a serious risk of twisting and tangling while you are fishing. Here is the right way to wind line on an open-face spinning reel. The spool with the new line should be held against the reel, so that the loops are wound off in the direction of the reel bail's rotation – namely, the same as the direction in which the line is wound onto the reel.

Left: The line should be of correct length, and evenly laid, on the spool. There is enough line when about 2 mm remain to the spool edge. Laying on more line will risk clumps of it coming off in the cast, while less line increases its friction against the spool edge and shortens the cast.

spinning reels are made according to the same principle, although the drag may be placed differently and the brake discs manufactured of different materials. The spool's form and the handle's way of folding may also vary.

The design of the reel handle makes it possible to retrieve the lure with either your left or right hand. The reel may also have a few, or many, ball bearings. The number of ball bearings is often a sellers' argument, but in fact there are many examples of reels with 3-4 bearings that last longer than others with 5-6 bearings.

The material of which the reel itself is made has varied in recent decades. Most reels were once made of aluminium, followed by graphite reels during the 1970s. These, however, were not very durable and the trend is now back toward aluminium reels, although graphite reels will continue in the low-price category.

Gearing

Today the majority of reels have a helical pinion, but some – mainly German ones – still have a worm pinion. This is a simple and practical design, which at first goes a little more sluggishly than a helical pinion but soon becomes "run in". To put it briefly, the worm pinion is a quite reliable gear that can last for years, and not a few have worked for 30 years.

The open-faced spinning reel is probably the world's most widespread type of reel. It is simple to handle – not least for beginners – and gives long, safe casts. Light lures from 2 to 10-15 grams also suit it very well. No matter whether the drag sits at its front or rear, this is an effective tool for tiring out even big fish.

Baitcasting reels

In contrast to spinning reels, the baitcasting reel has a rotating horizontal spool. The handle drives the spool by means of toothed wheels, whose gear ratio depends on the kind of fishing intended. Normally the ratio is around 5:1.

Granted that many of the modern small baitcasting reels are technical wonders, the basic principle of a baitcasting reel is elementary. But a certain amount of training is needed to cast with this reel. Despite its frequently well-planned brake system, beginners in particular are bound to suffer a backlash when the spool overwinds in the cast.

Prices are often much higher for baitcasting reels than for spinning reels. Like the latter, baitcasting reels of graphite were made during the 1980s, but time has shown that aluminium reel houses are best. In terms of design, there are two types of baitcasting reel: the classic cylindrical reel with round side-gables, and the more low-profiled variety. Both types have excellent mechanics and satisfy all the requirements of spinning and baitcasting.

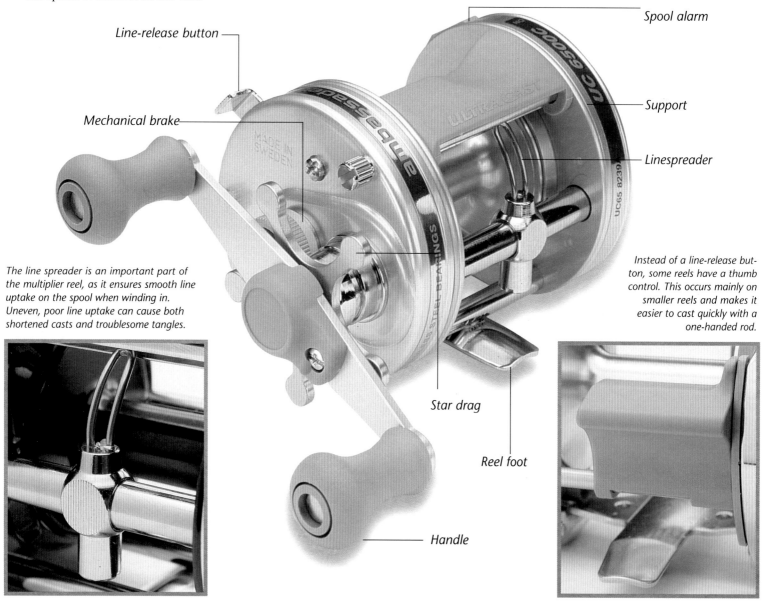

Line-release button

Spool alarm

Mechanical brake

Support

Linespreader

The line spreader is an important part of the multiplier reel, as it ensures smooth line uptake on the spool when winding in. Uneven, poor line uptake can cause both shortened casts and troublesome tangles.

Instead of a line-release button, some reels have a thumb control. This occurs mainly on smaller reels and makes it easier to cast quickly with a one-handed rod.

Star drag

Reel foot

Handle

Most multiplier reels today have effective cast-braking systems, both centrifugal and mechanical, to lessen the risk of running the spool too fast when casting.

When laying line onto a multiplier reel, the line's spool should be held so as to rotate in the same direction as the reel's spool. Stick a pencil into the line spool's mid-hole for smooth turning, and keep the line stretched between your fingers while laying on. The reel is full when 1-2 mm are left to its spool's upper edge.

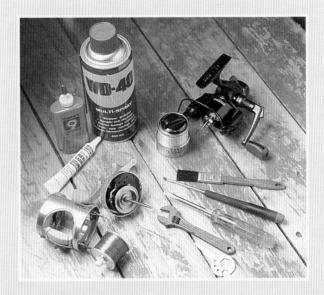

Care and maintenance

Reels can be damaged by salt water and dirty fresh water. Hence they should always be rinsed after a fishing trip, then dried and sprayed with silicon. Simultaneously the brakes should be loosened, as the discs may otherwise deform, making the reel's brake uneven and jerky. The handle knob and the bail springs should be given a couple of drops of oil, which will also benefit the line roller. With a baitcasting reel, you do yourself a service by putting a drop of oil on the screw. If the reel is used regularly, it should undergo a thorough service each year as well.

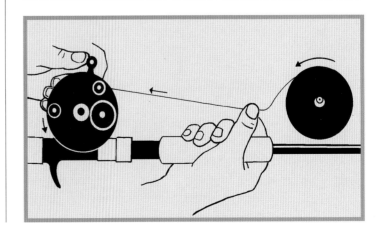

Lines

Nylon and monofilament lines are manufactured from a nylon raw material, consisting of tiny balls that are heated and pressed through holes of different sizes. The threads are then cooled over rollers that also stretch them, so that they become soft and elastic. Lines of good quality (and high price) are usually impregnated with waterproof substances, which settle between the nylon molecules and prevent the line from absorbing water – thus increasing the breaking strain. Lines can also be surface-treated with, for example, teflon. In sum, making a fishing line is not as simple as it may sound.

Knot strength and elasticity

Lines are often classified, meaning that you have a guarantee of the line breaking only at a certain load. But this raises the price, and such lines should not be bought unless you need to fish with them.

The best knots can provide a knot strength of 90-100 percent, while bad knots – or weaknesses in the knot itself – reach a knot strength of only 50-60 percent. Wear resistance also varies: some lines crack after a single snag on the bottom, or tear to pieces in the line guides after a few hours of fishing. Others, however, will last for many fishing days without a sign of weakness.

When you hook and fight a wild fish on a short line, elasticity is essential. But on a long line, lack of resilience is best. Some lines, in any case, stretch by at least 15-30 percent if they are wet. Generally, soft lines are more elastic than stiff ones.

It is always difficult to give good advice on which type of line to use, but the broad rule should be to choose soft lines for small reels. A stiff line does not lie so well on such a spool, and can easily lift off during the cast – perhaps resulting in a tangle. During cold and frost, it is best to fish with soft lines, since a stiff line then has a greater tendency to break.

Lines age at different rates. Sunlight, continual dampness, and chemicals can destroy a line. Neither should it come in contact with oil, mosquito spray, petrol and the like. Preferably store it in a dark place, and check it at regular intervals even while fishing. Especially the outermost metres of line are loaded hard during the cast, and by snags on the bottom, so they should be discarded before each new fishing trip.

Braided lines

The new braided multifilament lines are characterized by a very high breaking strain in relation to their diameter. They consist of many fibres, and were introduced by a German company that called its line Corastrong. The fibres, termed coramid, probably contain kevlar. Other, competing line manufacturers use fibres designated as spectra. Both of these line types, which are comparatively expensive, often come in blends with different fibre materials, to improve their knot strength and applicability.

These lines have rapidly won popularity, and will undoubtedly become even more widespread as their prices sink. Regarding cost, a common practice is to fill the reel partly with cheap nylon line, before winding on the expensive multifilament line.

The weak points of multifilament lines are the knots. One can recommend the Trilene knot, but a Uni-knot should be used for the nylon back-line. These lines also have certain weaknesses during frost, mainly due to ice formation.

Knots

No part of the spinning fisherman's "chain" of equipment is stronger than its weakest link – the knot. Incorrect or poorly tied knots can decrease the breaking strain by up to half. Still, there are dozens of knots that have survived for decades despite their weaknesses. The best approach is to learn three or four durable knots well, and thus be able to tie few but secure knots.

The spool, or arbor, knot comes in handy when the line is to be tied on the spool of a multireel or spinning reel. It is really just a simple three-turn clinch knot. The traditional clinch knot itself can be improved by giving the line an extra pass through the eye. This results in a so-called Trilene knot, with a breaking strain of 95-100 percent.

The right equipment

Water, species and fishing method, along with personal preference, determine an angler's fishing tackle.

Ultra-light fishing for small species calls for a short light rod, from 150-180 centimeters (4.5-6 feet) long, a small reel carrying a line capacity of 100-125 meters (108-135 yds), and a line diameter of 0.10-0.23 mm test strength. Choose a rod with a casting weight from 2 to 10 grams. This tackle is best

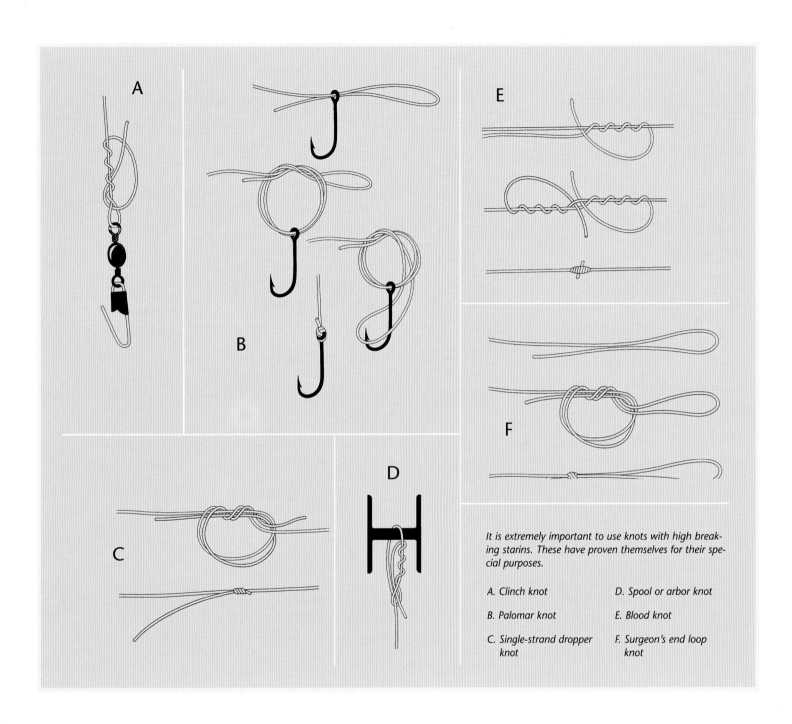

It is extremely important to use knots with high breaking starins. These have proven themselves for their special purposes.

A. Clinch knot

B. Palomar knot

C. Single-strand dropper knot

D. Spool or arbor knot

E. Blood knot

F. Surgeon's end loop knot

for fighting small trouts, bass and pikes. It is particularly suitable for boat fishing, for smaller ponds, rivers and streams.

Light spinning tackle is a supple rod about 6.5-7.5 feet long with a casting weight of 10-20 grams, a small reel and 0.23-0.30 mm diameter line. This is agood basic tackle combination that provides enormously satisfying fishing, but it is also

reliable when fishing for trout, bass, small pike or salmon. A lightweight rod with an extra long handle for two-handed casts gives extra strength and control.

A classic, all-round tackle consists of a rod of 7-9.5 feet with a casting weight of 12-28 grams (1/2-1 oz), a medium-sized reel and 150-180 meters of 0.25-0.35 mm diameter line.

Parts of the hook

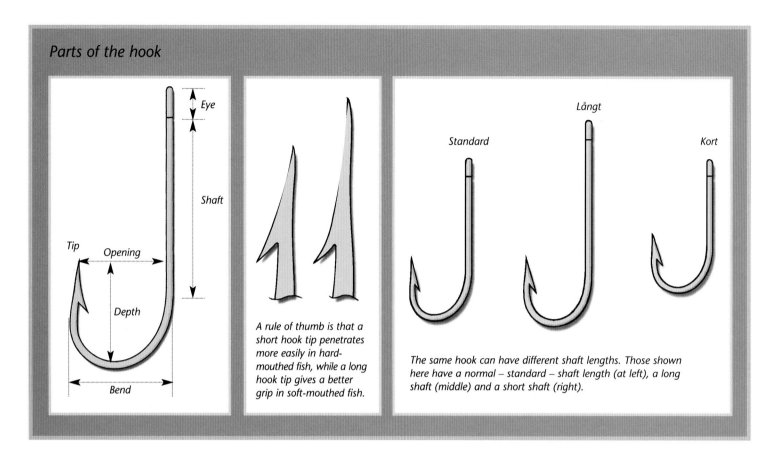

A rule of thumb is that a short hook tip penetrates more easily in hard-mouthed fish, while a long hook tip gives a better grip in soft-mouthed fish.

The same hook can have different shaft lengths. Those shown here have a normal – standard – shaft length (at left), a long shaft (middle) and a short shaft (right).

Hooks, swivels, rings and leaders

The hook is the light-tackle fisherman's most important detail, but it is often the piece of equipment given the least attention. What good are a rod, a reel, a line and lure that function as a perfect "casting machine" if the hook is weak, the point is not sharp enough, the connecting rings are weak—or if the fish can cut the line!

Hooks are available in more than 50,000 different shapes and sizes. They can be basically grouped as single, double or treble hooks. A single hook is commonly used with spoons, pirks and jigs, while double hooks are used sometimes with plugs. Treble hooks are the preferred hooks for artificial lures, even though they do not work as well as single hooks. When the force of a strike or of setting the hook is distributed over three points, none of them penetrate as well as when that same energy is concentrated in just one point. Experience has shown that treble hooks get more bites but lose more fish, while a single hook gets fewer bites but lands more fish.

Certain artificial lures are designed for fishing with either single or treble hooks, some even for double hooks. A jig is a traditional single hook lure, while plugs are traditionally treble hook lures.

The parts of a hook

The parts of a hook are the eye, the shank, the bend, the point, the gap and the barb. These parts can vary in shape and description, bearing names such as Hollow Point, Needle Eye, Kirbed Shank, and Reversed Point. In general, the names stick to the point—a round eye exactly that, a tapered eye has a tapered wire for an eye, and so on. Hooks with points curving inwards are usually [or natural bait and hooks with straight points are for spinning with artificials.

Hooks vary from size 28, only a few millimetres long, to size 18/0, which is a rugged shark hook. As the scale stretches from 28 down to 0, the hooks become large and larger, and as the scale progresses from 1/0 to 18/0 they continue to increase in size.

Hooks are made of wire of carbon, steel, or stainless steel. The wire is tempered in various ways so that some hooks are soft and some are hard. Some hooks are tin/nickel-plated for salt water, others are bronzed for use mainly in fresh water. Hooks can be coloured blue or red or gold. Blue or brown hooks provide camouflage; red hooks are used for red lures that look like boiled shrimp or the larvae of the mosquito *Ghironomidae*; gold hooks are used to make artificials extra attractive.

Most fresh factory hooks seem sharp and pointed at first glance, but the criterion for a sharp hook is if it can dig into a fingernail. If it cannot, it needs to be sharpened with either a whetstone or a file. Big hooks are sharpened with a file, smaller ones with a whetstone. After each strike or bottom snag the hook point should be checked and sharpened if necessary.

Split rings, swivels and snaps

Split rings, round or oval-shaped, are mounted either on the hook or the swivel. Oval connectors give the hook the most flexibility. This piece of equipment is usually the first bit of tackle to rust, so it is wise to keep a good supply in your tackle box.

A swivel is a thrust bearing used to connect the line and the lure. They were designed to eliminate the line twist that is commonly caused by rotating artificial lures. They come in many shapes and forms for different types of fishing. One special kind of swivel that is used with artificial lures has built-in ball-bearings to make it even more effective when trolling.

Snap swivels are used to make changing lures easier and faster. Once the snap is attached to the line, the lure can be changed by opening and closing the snap rather than tying a new knot. A snap, however, makes the lures more visible and even slightly heavier. The size of a snap should be kept to a minimum, especially when using small lures. A large snap can immobilize lightweight lures and perhaps make the fish skittish and suspicious. Snaps come in many shapes and sizes. Some are almost selflocking and are reliable when put under pressure, but others are weak. No-knot fast snaps are the very smallest snaps, designed for the quick changing of fliers or suspended lures.

Leaders

Leaders are not only for fishing predators with mouths full of sharp teeth. They are also useful when the last few meters of line are constantly being worn and abraded, when being dragged over rocks, boulders, branches and roots, i.e. when trolling. Casting is also hard on a line. Using a leader with a smaller diameter than the line makes the lure move more naturally. When fishing with a fluorescent line an effective technique is to use ordinary line which has less visibility on the one or two meters of line that are closest to the lure.

A leader is made either of strong monofilament or of several strands of wire that are covered with nylon. Pike, muskellunge and other fish with sharp teeth can fight and bite hard enough to damage the line or even to break it off. By tying a strong piece of line (25-40 cm with a breaking strain of 20-30 kg) at the end of the line, the fish has something to sink its teeth into.

Wire leaders are probably the most durable, but they are much more visible than nylon leaders. Both leaders can easilybe made yourself. A nylon leader requires a snap, a swivel and a suitable piece of line. A wire leader is made from sleeves, a swivel and a snap. A simple method of forming a loop in the end of a coated wire is to twist the tag end around the standing part of the coated wire 5-6 times and then heat itwith a match. Pre-tied leaders are available at all bait-and-tackle shops.

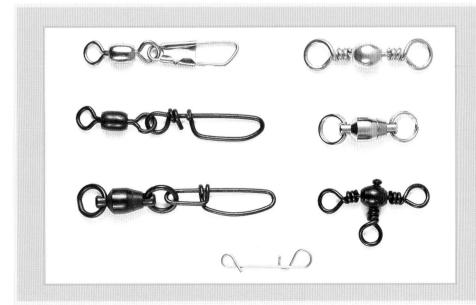

Swivels and snaps. (Left, from top:) Standard snap, Rosco snap, Berkley CrossLok. (Right, from top:) Standard swivel, Sampo ball-bearing swivel, three-way swivel. (Bottom:) A bait lock of the Not-a-knot type.

Casting Techniques

The ways of casting in practice are about as numerous as the fishermen who perform them. All of us develop our own casting style according to body build and equipment. But the rod's action and length are primary determinants of the casting method. Even competition casters have a special style of casting.

A cast involves a rapid acceleration of the rod – no matter whether you use a rod with one or two handles, and cast underhand or sideways. The technique cannot be taught as a theory: it must be learned by training. A bad cast is usually due to an unrhythmical or jerky casting movement. Thus a comfortable posture before the cast is important, and other circumstances play a role too. The leading types of cast are the overhead (overhand) and the side-cast.

The overhead cast

This precise technique begins by sighting at the target with the rod, from whose tip the bait hangs down 20-50 centimetres. The rod is brought behind your back, normally over the right shoulder, although some prefer to raise it over the left shoulder. Then the rod is accelerated forward over the same shoulder, aiming toward the target. A rod with top action needs slightly greater "sting" in the cast than a rod with whole action, which is little more than pushed upward during the forward movement.

The line is released when the rod is most flexed and points somewhat over the target. If the rod is well enough tensed in the cast, and if you have aimed exactly and let the line go at the right moment, you will hit the target. But if you release the line too soon, the bait will fly up in a high arc and fall in front of you. If released too late, the bait will strike the water before you like a projectile.

The overhead cast is not very easy to learn for a beginner, who often lets the line go too early or late. Neither is this cast safe when fishing from a boat, where you have difficulty in controlling a bait that hangs behind you. Nor does an overhead cast reach as far as a side-cast, which flexes the rod more and makes it travel farther.

An overhead cast can be performed with both a one-handed and a two-handed rod. In the latter case, the greatest transfer of energy is produced with the right hand, which controls the line release at the moment of casting and, simultaneously, pushes the rod forward. The longer and more powerful a rod is, however, the more pressure is given by the left hand, which is stretched backward. In really strong surf-casting rods, the left hand pushes most, while the right hand serves mainly for guidance.

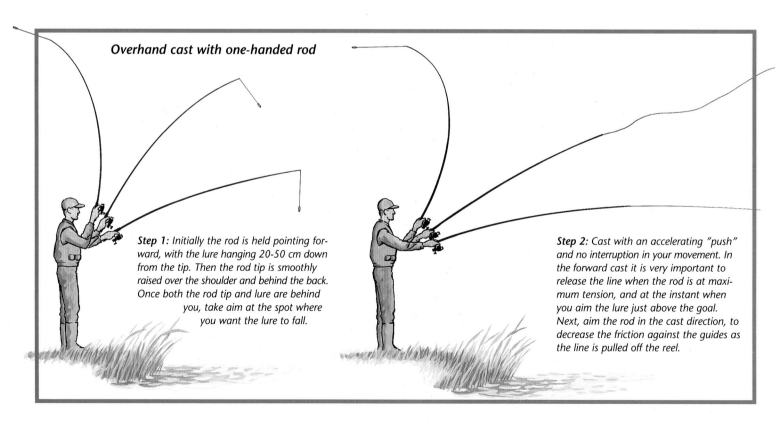

Overhand cast with one-handed rod

Step 1: Initially the rod is held pointing forward, with the lure hanging 20-50 cm down from the tip. Then the rod tip is smoothly raised over the shoulder and behind the back. Once both the rod tip and lure are behind you, take aim at the spot where you want the lure to fall.

Step 2: Cast with an accelerating "push" and no interruption in your movement. In the forward cast it is very important to release the line when the rod is at maximum tension, and at the instant when you aim the lure just above the goal. Next, aim the rod in the cast direction, to decrease the friction against the guides as the line is pulled off the reel.

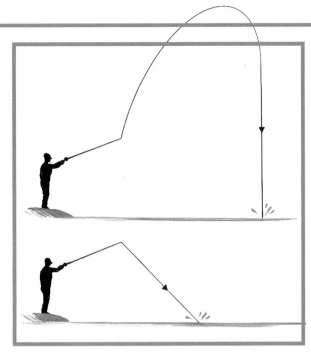

During the actual cast, the line must be able to shoot off the reel as easily and friction-free as possible. On a multiplier reel, the spool is released before starting the cast, and then your thumb is held against the spool until the line is to be let go. On a spinning reel, the bail arm is lowered with one hand while you lock the line with the other hand's forefinger or middle finger.

In all types of cast, releasing the line at the right moment is essential. If you release it too soon during an overhand cast, the lure will fly up in the air and fall a few metres away. If the release is delayed, the lure hits the water before your feet. In both cases the cast will be too short.

Overhand cast with two-handed rod

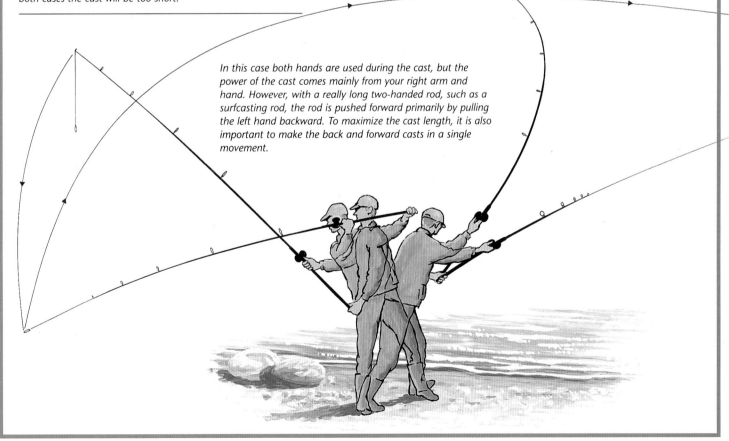

In this case both hands are used during the cast, but the power of the cast comes mainly from your right arm and hand. However, with a really long two-handed rod, such as a surfcasting rod, the rod is pushed forward primarily by pulling the left hand backward. To maximize the cast length, it is also important to make the back and forward casts in a single movement.

The side-cast

A side-cast is begun by bringing the rod horizontally backward. Depending on the rod's action, a forward acceleration is then made – still horizontally – and the rod is brought slightly upward, at which point the line is let out. Too early or late a release will send the bait flying to the right or left, respectively. You cannot aim with a side-cast, so it lacks precision, but it does yield greater force and a longer cast. In addition, the casting arc is longer than in an overhead cast, which means that the rod is flexed better. Even more flexing can be attained in the back cast, which continues in the forward cast, with a continuous movement that feels natural. This cast is excellent in a headwind, and the casting distance may be increased – if the rod's length and action permit – by having a little more line between the rod tip and the bait.

Side-casts are ideal for light spinning, where exact casting is not required. This cast is also often used from a boat, while sitting in the prow or stern to lay the casting arc outside the boat, without any danger for others aboard. Either a one-handed or a two-handed rod can be used to side-cast.

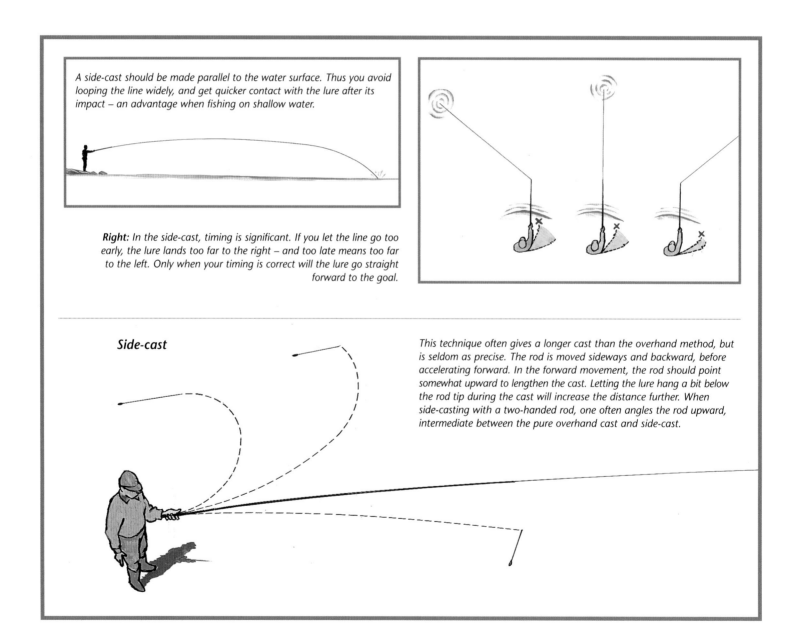

A side-cast should be made parallel to the water surface. Thus you avoid looping the line widely, and get quicker contact with the lure after its impact – an advantage when fishing on shallow water.

Right: *In the side-cast, timing is significant. If you let the line go too early, the lure lands too far to the right – and too late means too far to the left. Only when your timing is correct will the lure go straight forward to the goal.*

Side-cast

This technique often gives a longer cast than the overhand method, but is seldom as precise. The rod is moved sideways and backward, before accelerating forward. In the forward movement, the rod should point somewhat upward to lengthen the cast. Letting the lure hang a bit below the rod tip during the cast will increase the distance further. When side-casting with a two-handed rod, one often angles the rod upward, intermediate between the pure overhand cast and side-cast.

The pendulum cast

This is a short precision cast, and is best done with a spinning reel. The bait is started in a swinging movement with the free line, whose length may be from 30-50 centimetres to nearly the whole rod length. Once a fair swinging speed is reached, you aim at the target and release the line. Such a cast is used chiefly on confined waters surrounded by brushwood and branches, or wherever a cast of only a few metres is needed.

Left: The pendulum cast is very useful on minor waters with a high demand for precision. This photograph shows a typical situation: in the small deep holes are salmon, which have to get the lure presented properly with short but exact casts. Here the pendulum cast has the best chance of fishing the lure just where the fish are.

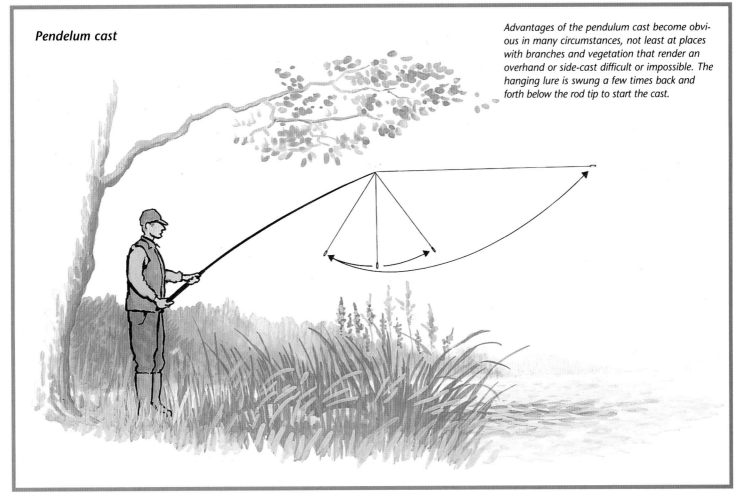

Pendelum cast

Advantages of the pendulum cast become obvious in many circumstances, not least at places with branches and vegetation that render an overhand or side-cast difficult or impossible. The hanging lure is swung a few times back and forth below the rod tip to start the cast.

Baits

Artificial lures can be divided into spoons, pirks, spinners, wobblers, jigs, and combinations of these, as well as plastic animals and flies. Each group includes thousands of variants. The types also differ in form, size, colour, weight and material. Spoons, pirks, spinners, and most jigs are sinking lures, but there are both sinking wobblers and floating ones. Within each group of lures, however, we can recognize the following main characteristics.

Spoons

Nearly all forms are found among spoons, but the majority have a real spoon- or S-shape. Their name is due to the fact that many of the first classic examples were spoon-like. Initially they were even fashioned from spoons – and few sportfishermen have avoided making a spoon out of just that utensil.

Both the spoon- and the S-shape hold these lures on course in the water. They should neither stray out to the sides, nor glide up to the surface when being retrieved. Their movement, besides the light, is also what enables the lures to send out reflections. Yet in principle only two types of spoon exist: broad, round and oval spoons – such as standard pike spoons – and long, thin spoons.

Broad spoons

A broad spoon moves slowly when it is retrieved at a normal rate. If the retrieval speed increases, the spoon begins to rotate and fishes ineffectively – a behaviour which is ever less pronounced for more slender spoons. The round and oval spoons imitate small fish, such as roach and crucian carp, while elongated spoons are imitations of smelt, bleak, sand lance, and small herring.

Generally, broad spoons are employed in still waters – for pike, perch and pikeperch – and have a calmly wobbling movement. Slender, elongated spoons are used in flowing waters and for coastal fishing. These do not wobble as much, and can be retrieved at high speed, or can stand quite motionless in the current and work. There are also spoons of thick sheet metal, which gives a longer cast, or of thin sheet that is more suitable for trolling.

Broad spoons. (From top, left to right:) Hammer, Ruggen, Pikko and Storauren, Crocodile Stubby, Atom, Moss Boss, Lillauren, Utö and Jurmo.

Weedguarded spoons. (From top:) Hobo, Atom Giller, Favorit Vass.

Weedless spoons

These spoons, usually of the broad type, are equipped with thin, stiff, single-strand wire that protects the hook. It is springy and thus exposes the hook to the fish when they bite. The hook shield prevents the hook from catching on weeds or other plants. Such spoons, therefore, are used only in areas with plenty of vegetation.

Their hooking abilities are, however, not the best, and this type of spoon involves a greater risk of losing the fish than do spoons without weedguards. Moreover, the hook is often fixed solidly to the spoon and cannot be replaced. Weedless spoons are designed mainly for pike fishing, and are to be retrieved in the same way as a broad spoon.

Certain large spoons in the class of 18-35 grams (1/2-1 ounce) are provided with two or three treble hooks, on the theory that they hook the fish better since it bites the lure crosswise. Practice has shown, however, that the line often hangs itself in the first hook or the middle hook, and that the fish is hooked better with only one treble hook.

Broad, round and oval spoons perform best, as a rule, at depths of 1-1.5 metres if they weigh 5-10 grams, at 1.5-2.5 metres if 10-20 grams, and at 2.5-5 metres if 20-35 grams. Only in clear water with vigorously hunting fish can you expect to succeed with spoons when the depth exceeds 5 metres.

Elongated spoons

Slender, thin and long spoons, with or without an S-bend, are imitations of fast-swimming fish. They are retrieved more rapidly than oval and round spoons, since a quick retrieval is just what they are intended for. Their primary use is in flowing waters, where retrieval is relatively slow and the current makes the spoon look alive. They are also used in coastal fishing for marine fish such as sea trout, cod and mackerel. The marine species that take elongated spoons are often fast swimmers with a slender body form.

This type of spoon was originally moulded in lead. But lead

Fishing with broad spoons

A broad spoon is ideal for any kind of spinning in lakes and in the calmer parts of waterways – for perch, pike, musky and pikeperch. Use the countdown method, and let the spoon sink almost to the bottom before starting to retrieve. The spinning speed is correct when you notice the lure's movements in the rod tip. Vary the speed with spin-stops and a slow or rapid retrieval. Bear in mind that a predatory fish normally takes the lure during a spin-stop, and often when the line is slack.

As long as the spoon moves in deep water, it is retrieved with the rod tip lowered. When it enters shallow water, the rod tip should be lifted. Thus you keep closer contact with the spoon and can control its deep movements better. Some spoons have a built-in pattern of uneven movement: during retrieval, they lurch through the water but stray to one side at regular intervals. This unpredictable gait can make the spoon a true "killer".

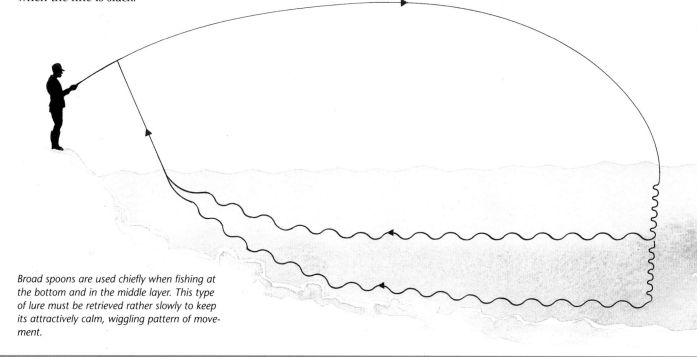

Broad spoons are used chiefly when fishing at the bottom and in the middle layer. This type of lure must be retrieved rather slowly to keep its attractively calm, wiggling pattern of movement.

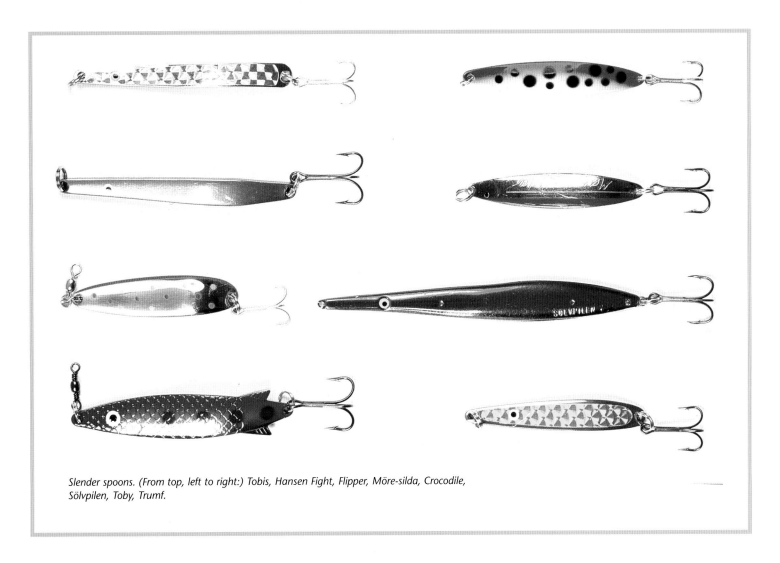

Slender spoons. (From top, left to right:) Tobis, Hansen Fight, Flipper, Möre-silda, Crocodile, Sölvpilen, Toby, Trumf.

is a soft material, so the finish is not very durable on these spoons, or on pirks, whose painting and lacquer flake off when they hit rocks. Some lead-moulded pirks do have hard lacquer, yet it easily cracks if they hit rocks or snag on the bottom.

The drawback of lead-moulded pirks is that they are compact and heavy in comparison with their size. They cast well, but must be retrieved rapidly to avoid settling firmly on the bottom. The lead-moulded spoons and pirks that are produced today, though, have a larger bearing surface and less elongation than previously. For environmental reasons, lead-moulded lures will probably disappear from the market in time.

During recent decades, such small lead-moulded spoons and pirks have been gradually replaced by spoons made of iron or brass sheet. Some of these are straight and have a linear gait in the water. Others have a slight S-bend and are retrieved more slowly. This type of spoon combines the best properties of the earlier lead-moulded pirks with a more lively, attractive movement. Its elongated form also allows a fine cast. The spoon's rear part is often a little wider or heavier than its front part.

Elongated spoons do not twist the line as readily as the oval and round spoons. Their hooking abilities are excellent, too. Spoons of 5-15 grams are used at depths of 1-1.5 metres, 10-20 grams at 1.5-3 metres, and 20-35 grams at 3-5 metres.

Fishing with elongated spoons

Elongated spoons are meant to catch fast-swimming fish in waters with wide surfaces – such as sea trout, cod, garfish and mackerel along coasts, or trout in lakes. Just as with broad spoons, the countdown method is employed when retrieving, if the predatory fish are holding on the bottom. Usually, however, they circulate in the middle layer or at the surface.

Its design makes this type of spoon best for rapid retrieval, when it imitates species like smelt, sand lance, and bleak that swim intermittently through the water. Repeated spin-stops and a varied speed of retrieval are also important when fishing with such lures. During spin-stops, a well-balanced spoon will sink horizontally and rotate around its own axle.

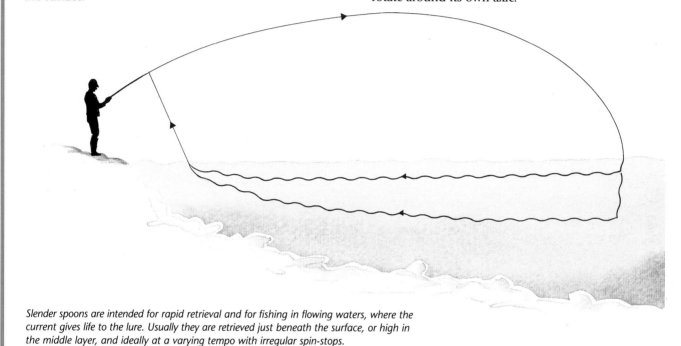

Slender spoons are intended for rapid retrieval and for fishing in flowing waters, where the current gives life to the lure. Usually they are retrieved just beneath the surface, or high in the middle layer, and ideally at a varying tempo with irregular spin-stops.

Pirks

A pirk (alternatively called a pilk, metal casting jig, diamond jig, or jigging spoon) may weigh from 40-50 up to 500 grams, when used in marine fishing for cod, pollack, cusk, mackerel and other predators. Pirks were originally a Scandinavian lure, employed by professional fishermen to catch cod. This group is very big, including hundreds of types and sizes, but generally they can be divided into light pirks for casting in shallow water (5-20 metres) and heavy pirks for casting in deeper water.

Some pirks are still made of lead and, being heavy and compact, serve very well in deep water, where the current is strong and the boat drifts fast. Other pirks, with a larger surface, are manufactured of brass or iron. These are livelier, for calm and less demanding conditions such as still or shallow water. The line thickness also influences the choice of pirk. So-called braided lines, based on spectra or kevlar, with a small diameter relative to their strength, enable one to use a lighter pirk.

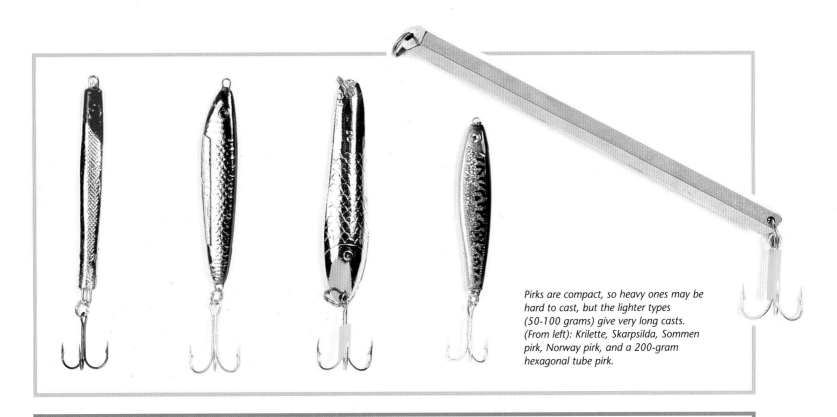

Pirks are compact, so heavy ones may be hard to cast, but the lighter types (50-100 grams) give very long casts. (From left): Krilette, Skarpsilda, Sommen pirk, Norway pirk, and a 200-gram hexagonal tube pirk.

Fishing with pirks

The lighter pirks are intended for casting on deeper water, often from a boat. They are retrieved in a jerky, varied manner – either on the bottom, where cod and cusk are found, or in the middle layer with its pollack and mackerel. During retrieval, one must also take account of the depth and the boat's drift, normally casting in the direction of drift.

Heavy pirks come into play for pirk fishing, or vertical fishing. Here the pirk is sunk to the bottom, and then the reel is coupled in. The rod's up-and-down movements give vitality to the otherwise compact pirk. In deep water and strong currents, pirk fishing requires you to have constant contact with the bottom, so that the pirk does not lift off it.

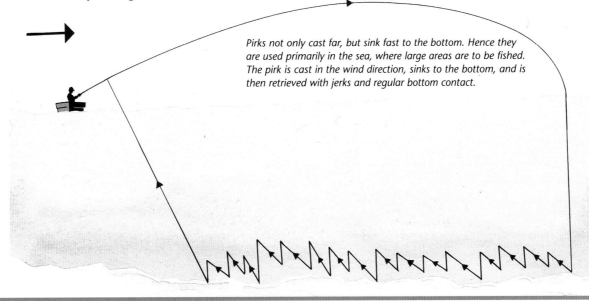

Pirks not only cast far, but sink fast to the bottom. Hence they are used primarily in the sea, where large areas are to be fished. The pirk is cast in the wind direction, sinks to the bottom, and is then retrieved with jerks and regular bottom contact.

Spinners

A spinner has the simple structure of a spoon that rotates around a wire or body, and moves straight in the water. It is actually amazing that so many predatory fish are tempted by spinners, which do not resemble any fish – as spoons and wobblers do. The spinner's body stays still while the spoon turns and gives it life. Moreover, the spinner continually sends out reflections, and the vibrations from the spoon attract fish. Numerous fish species that never take spoons or wobblers can be drawn to a spinner, such as various whitefish species.

Standard spinners

A standard spinner is made from a stiff, single-strand wire with a loop at each end, one for the hook and one to tie the line on. All spinners have a body, except some that are intended for very shallow water. In front of the body are a bead and a bend in which the spoon is mounted. The bead, made of plastic of metal, provides a light gait and minimizes friction between the body and the rotating spoon.

It is essentially the spinner body's size and weight that, together with the spoon's form, determine which waters and depths the spinner is suitable for. A heavy body is able to spin in deep water and strong currents. A light body, for example on the classic Mepps spinner, gives a superficial gait that is most effective in shallow and slow waters.

The spoon's construction reveals how the spinner moves in the water. A short, broad spoon rotates slowly, so the spinner travels high, which is good for fishing in shallows. Such a spoon rotates more vertically in relation to the body, too. If you want to fish deeper with this type of spinner, it cannot be done with a bigger and heavier spinner of the same type, since the spoon creates a correspondingly greater lifting force and keeps the spinner at the same depth. Instead, you must choose a spinner with a relatively heavier body, or with a thinner and longer spoon, which will not only go deeper but can be retrieved faster.

A spinner works superbly on most predatory fish, but is less effective in cold water. For it must go at a certain speed if the spoon is to rotate, and thus often runs too high for fish in cold water.

A further variation is seen in spinners with a feather hackle

Standard spinners.
(From above): Lindy Big Fish, Musky Killer.

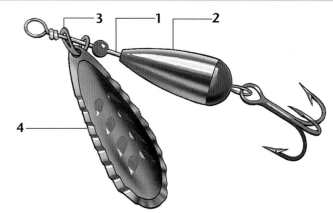

Regardless of the spoon's shape and the spinner body's design, the basic construction is the same: a rotating spoon that emits sound waves, which predatory fish interpret as small fish fleeing. A spinner's parts are the wire axle (1), spinner body (2), wire bail (3) and spinner spoon (4).

around the treble hook. Large "bucktail" spinners, with a dense skirt of deer hair there, are used for musky fishing. Alternatively, an octopus skirt on the treble hook can obtain the same effect. This yields a long, billowy, enticing spinner with a

total length of about 20 centimetres (8 inches). Standard spinners are meant for fishing in shallow or medium-depth waters, down to 3 metres.

Fishing with standard spinners

The majority of standard spinners are relatively light lures that sink slowly and do not cast very far. If you start the retrieval with a jerk on the rod tip, you can be sure that the spinner rotates, but you often feel it through the weight or resistance on the rod tip.

A standard spinner is fine for flowing waters, where it can even be made to stay at the same spot in the current, and to rotate and work at different tempos. If the current is too strong, though, the spinner will lift toward the surface. These spinners are most attractive if you avoid spin-stops but vary the retrieval speed and keep the spoon rotating.

Again, the spinner is excellent for retrieving near the bottom – in both still and flowing waters. But as soon as its resistance to the rod tip disappears, the spoon's rotation will have collapsed. By lifting the rod tip or retrieving a little faster, you can restart the rotation. Thus, the spinner's resistance on the rod allows you to check that it is working properly, and make it go just as slowly or as near the bottom as you want.

In flowing water, a spinner is usually considered best for fishing downstream. However, spinning upstream is a quite effective method, as the spinner approaches the fish like a natural prey.

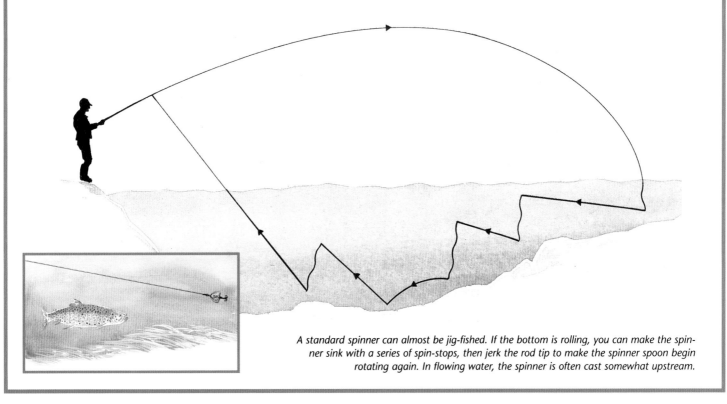

A standard spinner can almost be jig-fished. If the bottom is rolling, you can make the spinner sink with a series of spin-stops, then jerk the rod tip to make the spinner spoon begin rotating again. In flowing water, the spinner is often cast somewhat upstream.

Wobblers (plugs)

In contrast to spoons and spinners, which look like small fish only from particular angles, a wobbler is three-dimensional. Most plugs today are made of plastic, but balsa wood was once common. Plugs of balsa are still used to some extent, and many sportfishermen consider these more lively.

If you compare a balsa and a plastic plug with the same appearance and form, the balsa plug displays a lot more vitality. However, it is less durable and often suffers damage from fish teeth and impacts. Plugs are fantastic lures for pike, trout, salmon, musky, perch, and a long list of salt-water species. There are innumerable plugs which can float, sink, deep-dive, "hover" or serve for trolling. Some are also made for fishing right in the surface.

Floating plugs

Most plugs float, which means that they have a lower specific weight than water does. Thus, a plug floats because it is filled with air chambers or bubbles. The majority of wooden plugs, too, can float. A plug is provided with a "bill" or lip (or jaw-spoon) of metal or plastic, which makes it dive or cut down through the water when being retrieved. This bill is fixed on most plugs, but on a few it is adjustable so that the plug can descend to different depths. Some plugs are two-part constructions, and have a more lively slithering gait.

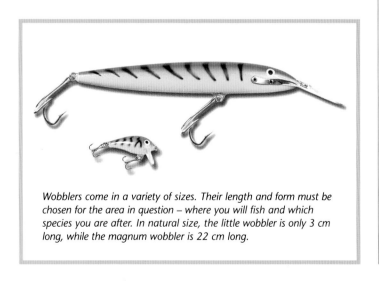

Wobblers come in a variety of sizes. Their length and form must be chosen for the area in question – where you will fish and which species you are after. In natural size, the little wobbler is only 3 cm long, while the magnum wobbler is 22 cm long.

Wobbterm

Floating wobblers.
From top left to right: Down Deep Rattlin Rap, Ukko Tipsy, Invincible, Tobimarv.

From top: *Clown, Crawdad, Firetige.*

Suspending wobblers: Husky Jerk and Suspending Rattlin' Rouge.

Suspending wobblers

These wobblers have the same density as water, and thus neither sink nor float, so one can make them "hover" freely at any desired level. They maintain this depth even during long spin-stops and extremely slow retrieval. Fishing with such wobblers may be very effective when the fish are sluggish and hard to catch.

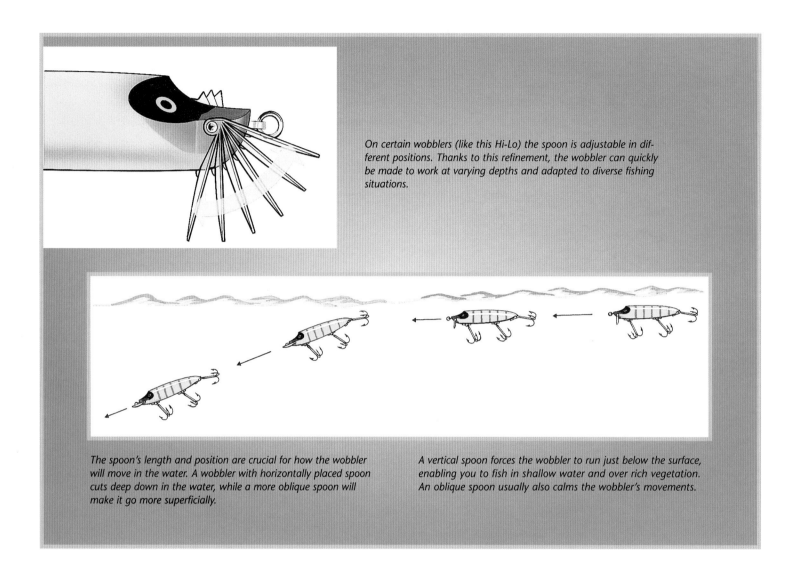

On certain wobblers (like this Hi-Lo) the spoon is adjustable in different positions. Thanks to this refinement, the wobbler can quickly be made to work at varying depths and adapted to diverse fishing situations.

The spoon's length and position are crucial for how the wobbler will move in the water. A wobbler with horizontally placed spoon cuts deep down in the water, while a more oblique spoon will make it go more superficially.

A vertical spoon forces the wobbler to run just below the surface, enabling you to fish in shallow water and over rich vegetation. An oblique spoon usually also calms the wobbler's movements.

The plug's bill, in combination with the retrieval speed, determines how deeply it can dive and whether it wobbles little or much in the water. If the bill is small, the plug moves relatively little, but a large bill makes the plug livelier. If the bill lies almost horizontally, the plug will cut deep into the water, while a more transverse bill gives the plug a calmer gait. With a nearly vertical bill, the plug goes slowly and almost in the surface. In addition, some plugs have an adjustable metal bill that can be bent up or down to change the degree of diving.

Other forms of adjustment exist to influence the movement of a floating plug. For example, some plugs have two knot eyes, the upper one producing a deep gait and the lower one a more superficial gait. The plug may also be weighted with lead, a bit up on the line, so that it can go deeper. The Rapala or Duncan knot is common on small, finely balanced plugs. A fixed knot, tied high in the plug's eye, deepens its dive somewhat. If the fixed knot is slid down as far as possible in the eye, the plug will go more superficially. However, floating plugs are always limited as regards their fishing depths, due of course to their specific weight in comparison with water.

Many plugs are equipped with two or three treble hooks. By removing one or two of these – or substituting, for instance, thinner hooks – the plug acquires a lighter and livelier gait.

Fishing with floating plugs

The faster a plug is retrieved, the deeper it goes. But the rod tip must be kept low. In the last part the retrieval, the plug will wander up toward the surface, and then it is especially important to hold the rod tip down at the water.

Most floating plugs are intended to fish at depths of 1-6 metres. Since they float, numerous spin-stops will let them ascend toward the surface and – as the retrieval continues – dive again. This is a very effective technique

A floating wobbler that is weighted can be fished just over the bottom, even in strong current and at relatively great depth. Too short a line between the three-way swivel and the lure, though, can worsen the wobbler's lively gait.

for retrieving them. In cold water, though, floating plugs are not so effective, since they demand a reasonable speed of movement in order to work at the bottom – and this speed is often too high, so a sinking plug or a lead-weighted floating plug is more effective.

In flowing waters, a floating plug has two advantages. It can be allowed to drift with the current down to an assumed holding place, and then be retrieved. Moreover, you can stop during the retrieval so that the plug soars over submerged obstacles such as plants and stones.

Floating, deep-diving plugs are recognizable by their frequently compact body, but also by the extra-long bill which makes the plug cut down to depths of 3-8 metres. On the other hand, a plug requires a certain retrieval speed if it is to reach maximum depth. Too slow a retrieval leads the plug to work inefficiently; and if you retrieve too fast, it will cut out in the water.

This type of plug is quite good at depths of 3-6 metres – and extremely effective for searching slopes at 3-7 metres, where it often hits the bottom and creates sounds that attract pikeperch, walleye and perch. The large versions of these plugs are mainly devoted to trolling for pike, musky and saltwater species.

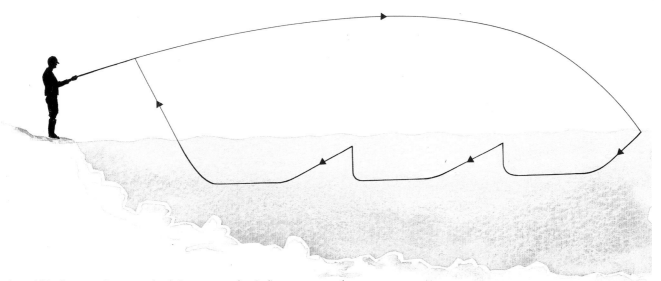

The wobbler floats on the water after being cast out, but it dives as soon as the retrieval begins. During spin-stops, it will rise toward the surface, working down again when the retrieval resumes.

Fishing with sinking plugs

The speed of descent varies among sinking plugs. Small sizes are intended for depths of 2-3 metres, and the larger plugs can be used down to 8-10 metres, but it often takes at least half a minute for the plug to reach the bottom. You should thus use the countdown method for this type of plug.

When the retrieval is begun, the plug will slowly lift from the bottom. Hence, numerous spin-stops are important to make it stay at the bottom, where most predatory fish linger. You may then need to release a little line regularly, by switching over the bail on a spinning reel or disengaging the spool on a multiplier reel.

Sinking plugs are better than floating ones for fishing in cold water, since they can be retrieved slowly.

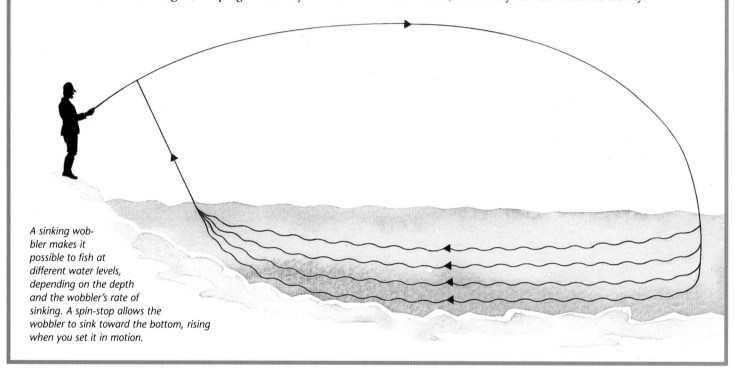

A sinking wobbler makes it possible to fish at different water levels, depending on the depth and the wobbler's rate of sinking. A spin-stop allows the wobbler to sink toward the bottom, rising when you set it in motion.

Sinking plugs

A floating plug cannot, unless it is weighted, be used with the countdown method at great depths. Here the sinking plug is better suited. Such a plug is normally made of plastic, having no air chambers or bubbles. The plastic may either be denser than water or contain weighting. Wooden plugs also exist in sinking versions.

Usually the package shows whether the plug is sinking (S) or floating (F), but you can often tell the difference by feeling its weight in your hand. As with most floating plugs, the depth-going of a sinking plug depends on the bill's size, placement, and cleavage of the water, besides the location of the knot eyes. The plug can be adjusted, too, by changing the bill or replacing the hooks. A few deep-going plugs with a long bill can work down to 7 metres.

Sinking wobblers. (From above, left to right:)
Rapala Countdown, Jawbreaker, Canadian Wiggler, Cisco Kid, Hi-Lo, Hi-Lo
Jointed, Rattlin' Rapala, Sliver, Shad Rap, Zalt, Hi-Lo Minnow Jointed.

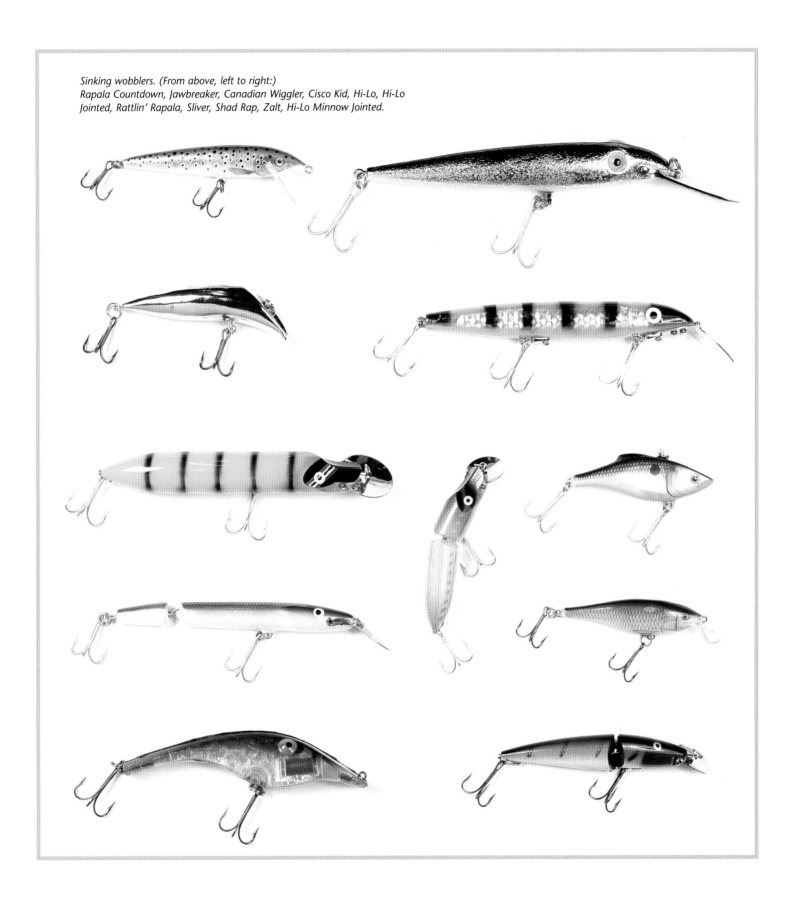

Jigs

The jig belongs to the classic artificial baits in American bass fishing. Although occasional jigs appeared on the European fishing scene during the 1960s, only in the 1970s did they really enjoy a breakthrough for pike and pikeperch fishing. Then they became an increasingly common option to other lures in, for example, trout fishing at rivers and lakes – and next for fishing in shallow marine waters. This is strange, as there can hardly be any cheaper or better artificial bait than a jig, which long ago was included in the survival gear of various fleets together with hooks, lines and other emergency accessories.

Normal lures, such as spoons and plugs, have built-in patterns of movement. The jig is different. At first sight, it looks most like a lump of lead with a tuft of feathers or plastic and an upturned single hook. In spite of that, there are diverse designs of American jigs – and some forms go back to the 1920s and 1930s. The keel and projectile types are intended for flowing waters, where the jig's shape makes it cut downward. The ball types are meant for spinning in still waters, while the banana and mushroom types apply to light jig fishing from a boat and to fishing in deep water.

Some jigs also carry a long bill. In this respect they resemble a plug, but the jig lacks the plug's ability to cut down into the water. Other jigs are provided with propellers or small rotor blades. The knot eye – which is the hook eye as well – may have a forward orientation to keep plants off the hook. But most jigs have the eye on top of the lead head, which is moulded around the hook. The latter is nearly always of Aberdeen type and browned, gilded or nickel-plated.

Jigs with a rubber body are cheap to work with, since you can buy replaceable bodies for them. However, some toothed predatory fish can destroy a rubber body in no time. If you get a bad bite or the fish is difficult to hook, it may be because the jig body is too long – but a body made of hair, feathers or rubber can be shortened with a knife or scissors to facilitate hooking. Rubber jigs are best stored in tackle boxes marked "Wormproof", which prevent certain chemicals in the rubber bodies from smearing off, or melting both the bodies and the box's plastic. Bodies of each colour should be kept in a separate plastic bag. This will also keep them from drying out.

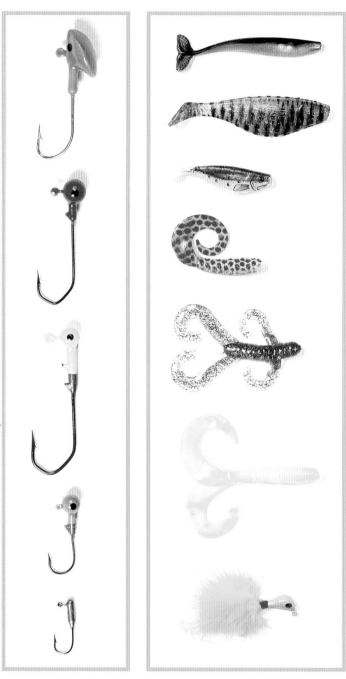

Above left: Jig heads come in a range of colours, forms, sizes and weights. Some common variants of jig heads are round, oval, tubular, banana-shaped, keel-shaped and conical. The hook's appearance may also differ according to the area, and to the type of jig body it is intended for.

Above right: The jig was originally the typical bass lure, but many people now consider jigs effective for diverse species in both fresh and marine waters. A jig's lively plastic tail enables it to be fished in very slowly without losing its attractiveness. Despite its simple design, it works fine in most fishing situations.

Fishing with jigs

All of the lures discussed previously are retrieved. But a jig has to be both "worked" and retrieved. The jig itself is dead, and the fisherman must bring it alive with rod and wrist movements during the retrieval. Vigorous jerks along the bottom are needed – whether long tempting jerks, or short chopping jerks, depending on the kind of fish you are after. Correct use of a jig is certainly a craft, but it can yield great satisfaction in the right hands.

Maintain continuous contact with the jig, but do not stretch the line so much as to affect the jig's gait. Make a strike at the least suggestion of a take. In contrast to spoons, plugs and other lures, it is quite common that a jig's construction attracts cautious nibbles without hook-ing the fish. Apart from flies, almost no other type of artificial bait is in such close touch with the fish at the taking stage. Many people believe that a jig is suited only to fishing on hard bottoms without vegetation; but if there is any vegetation, you should use an ultra-light jig that bounces off the plants. The hook does not snag, since it is turned upward.

Jigs have many practical advantages. Their aerodynamic shape gives long casts even in a headwind, and the compact head allows exact casts as well as good bottom contact. Moreover, a jig cuts down into the current better, so it is easier to keep in contact with the bottom than are other types of lure.

Jigs are primarily used for fishing along the bottom. Retrieval should be varied, and the jig fished in with alternately short and long jerks of the rod, so that it "hops" across the bottom. When fishing in flowing waters, the jig is cast across them or obliquely downstream, and retrieved with small tugs. A good presentation technique is essential if the jig is to behave irresistibly.

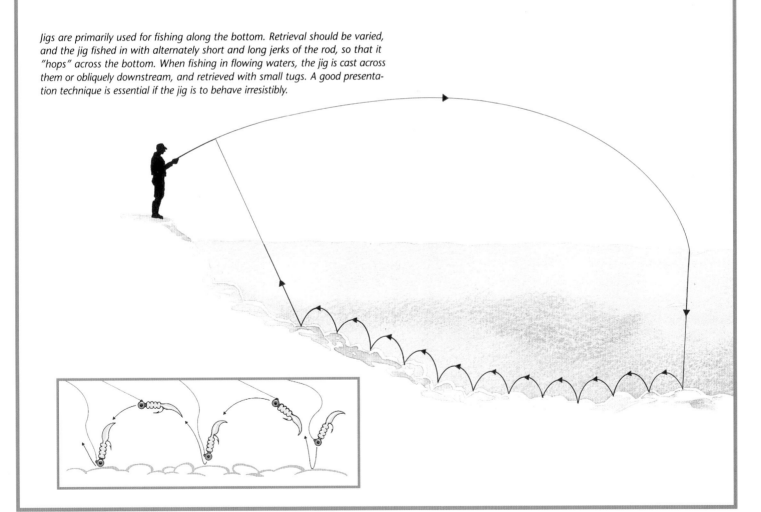

Casting floats

There are occasions in spinning when a spoon, plug or spinner is too large a lure for the predatory fish and, for example, a fly is much more suitable. Especially salmon in many waters can be so shy and cautious that big lures do not work. The diminished appetite for large bait may be due to the water temperature or level, insect hatchings, the season, spawning or other conditions.

An alternative is then to spin with flies in the surface, aided by a casting float. This device comes in two basic versions. One, the Bonnand type, is shaped like a cigar, with a red top, and contains lead as a weight. It is filled with air and can also be used as an ordinary float. At each end is a hole to tie the main line or the leader in.

The other version is the classic plastic "bubble", or Buldo. A transparent or colourful ball with two knot eyes, it can be opened via two small rubber valves and filled with water – the casting weight – so that it floats exactly in the surface. Also available are oval variants to be filled with water.

The fly should be on the end of a leader 1.0-4.5 metres long. Many sportfishermen use a permanently fixed leader, which is tied to a casting bubble. There are two kinds of sliding leader. The first is a 50-cm length of 0.40-mm line, inserted through the bubble and provided with a swivel at each end for the leader or main line. When the fish takes the fly during retrieval, you thus have 50 cm of "loose line" which the fish can pull out together with the fly. The second kind, used when you want to give more "loose line", is made by ending the leader with a swivel, to which the main line is tied after being inserted through the casting bubble. This swivel serves as a stopper.

Casting floats essentially function as casting weights. In recent years, however, different sorts of casting weights have been introduced. These are normally made of plastic or wood, with casting weights built or moulded into them. They are used in the same way as casting floats – with both a fixed and a sliding leader.

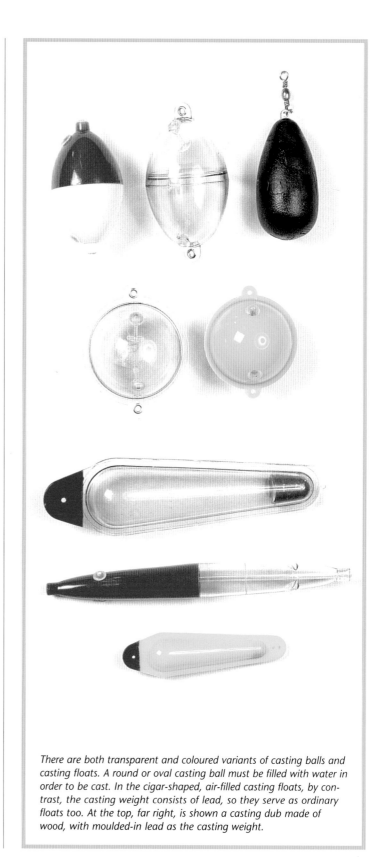

There are both transparent and coloured variants of casting balls and casting floats. A round or oval casting ball must be filled with water in order to be cast. In the cigar-shaped, air-filled casting floats, by contrast, the casting weight consists of lead, so they serve as ordinary floats too. At the top, far right, is shown a casting dub made of wood, with moulded-in lead as the casting weight.

Fishing with casting floats

To fish with a long leader and an often heavy casting weight, you need a relatively long, strong rod and a line of 0.25-0.35 mm. The cast is carried out when the leader lies in front of the fisherman in the water – never behind. Retrieval should be slow with many pauses, depending on which species of fish you are after. A lot of sportfishermen dislike this method, since the fishing is monotonous and may even be boring. But there is no doubt of its effectiveness.

Plastic bubbles can be weighted so much that they sink. In some put-and-take fishing, weighted "neutral" and "sinking"

bubbles are frequently used at depths as great as 5-8 metres.

If you want to fish deep with a fly, you can weight the leader with lead shot, or perhaps tie a piece of fast-sinking flyline into the leader.

The strike should be delivered with a smooth, controlled movement, because the plastic bubble gives quite a resistance in the water. Beginners have a habit of making too hard a strike, which results in the line breaking at the bubble.

Casting floats are useful in both still waters and rivers, where they enable a fly to fish just as well as the flyfisherman's floating line with a fly.

Fishing with a sliding leader means that the fish is given a little loose line when it takes. The two swivels function as stops, both when retrieving (left) and when the fish has taken the lure (right). Many think that a permanently mounted leader gives better hooking, but that the contact with lure and fish is improved by a sliding leader.

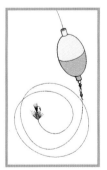

Right: Shown here are three methods of mounting a casting float on the line. Above is a permanent mounting, and below it are two variants with a sliding line.

Below: In Scandinavia, fishing with long-casting balls has become a frequent – and rewarding – way to present traditional flies for coastal sea trout.

Spinning with flies

Spinning does not by any means rule out the possibility of using flies in deep water. If the fly is weighted slightly up on the line, it can be fished at depth in both still and flowing water. In Scandinavia the so-called "spinning-fly" method is thus applied to trout, salmon and seagoing trout in streams and rivers. However, this has angered flyfishermen and been forbidden in many places due to its effectiveness.

The leader is 1-1.5 metres long, of 0.20-0.40 mm line, depending on whether trout in small rivers or salmon and sea trout in large rivers are fished. It is tied in a three-way swivel, the distance to the sinker being 20-30 cm long. The choice of fly is not very difficult. Ordinary trout flies serve for all forms of trout fishing, while double-hooked flies or tube flies are used for salmon and sea trout.

Lagging flies

It often happens that a predatory fish pursues a plug, spoon or spinner without biting – no matter what type of bait or retrieval technique is used. In this case, a "lagging" fly offers both an alternative and a surprising arrangement that can trick the fish. You simply knot a fly in a short or long leader on a spoon, plug or spinner, after removing the hook(s).

Char is a typical fish species that gladly takes a lagging fly. Perch, pike, trout, and garfish in salt water, too, respond positively to it. But the fly tends to get hung up in the main line when casting against the wind, so a lagging – or perhaps "persistent" – fly should be used only in calm weather or with the wind at your back.

Droppers

Droppers are flies, plastic animals, or micro-jigs that are tied to the line above the lure. They markedly increase the chances of catching fish, since many predators are curious and often become "envious" when they see a little fish being chased by a bigger one. Perch, trout and bass, as well as marine species like sea trout, mackerel and cod, readily take droppers. The droppers are tied in a leader 30-50 cm over the main lure, and it is frequently only to them that the fish reacts.

Spinning with a fly can yield fine catches in rivers with salmon and sea trout. This salmon could not resist a weighted tube fly, fished at the bottom.

Fishing with spinning flies

Spinning with a fly in flowing water can be done exactly as with a spoon. All the fishing is oriented directly or obliquely downstream, so that the fly swings in toward your own bank. By paying out line or lifting the rod, you can make the fly work deeper or higher. During this process, you regularly raise and lower the rod to "pump" the fly in: it more or less zigzags against the current as it approaches your bank.

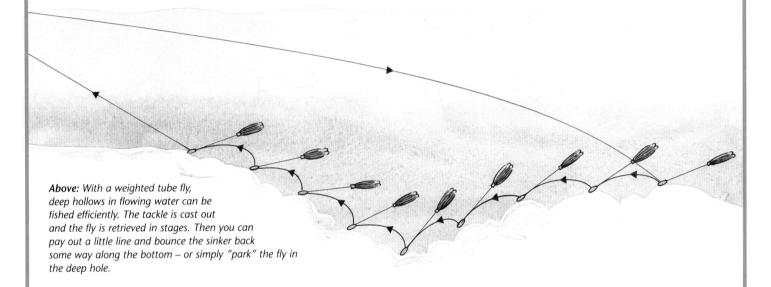

Above: With a weighted tube fly, deep hollows in flowing water can be fished efficiently. The tackle is cast out and the fly is retrieved in stages. Then you can pay out a little line and bounce the sinker back some way along the bottom – or simply "park" the fly in the deep hole.

The spinning fly can be weighted by attaching the sinker to the main line, either directly or via a leader. The leader, which should be thinner than the main line, is then fastened in a swivel or three-way snap. But the line between the swivel and fly must have the same breaking strength as the main line.

It is not unusual for predatory fish to become "envious" when they see a smaller fish hunted by bigger ones, and this reaction is what makes the dropper an effective attractor. A dropper is normally attached to a leader 30-50 cm above the lure. Likewise, a fly dragged after the lure can attract a bite, but the leader should then be only about 10 cm long.

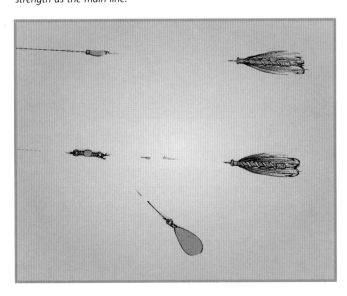

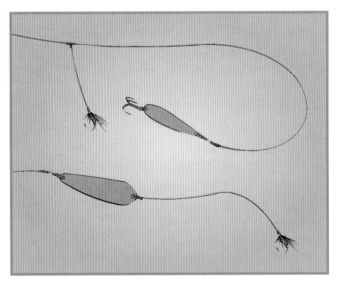

Jerkbait

No other spinning technique is as demanding as jerkbait-fishing. When mastered, it also gives the greatest rewards in terms of spectacular takes and, under certain conditions, efficient catches.

Jerkbait-fishing has long been an established technique for pike and musky in North America. Since the early 1990s, its fame has also spread across most of pike-crazy Europe. The name comes, of course, from jerking the bait. Unlike a plug, whose nose-bill gives it a gait, a jerkbait has no bill and is dependent on the "life" that the fisherman gives it.

Technique

The fisherman stands up, casts out, points the rod straight toward the bait, and brings it home by jerking downward with the rod. After each jerk, the arc of line that has been created is wound in, and the rod is moved back to the starting position, until the line is stretched again and the fisherman makes a new jerk. Short and sharp jerks, or slow and spaced jerks, give the bait different kinds of behavior. Preferably the fisherman should maintain a certain rhythm. A jerkbait is designed so that, with a good rhythm, it swims in a zigzag, gliding to one side at each jerk and to the other side at the next jerk.

Since the technique relies on the fisherman's ability to jerk the rod toward the water surface without hitting it, jerk rods are short. They are also stiff, for casting weights up to 150 grams, so that the jerks will be transferred to the bait. As a friend said of somebody else's jerk rod, it's "soft as a broomstick". In order to hook the fish with such a short rod and not lose anything from the movement, the fishing is done with inelastic braided lines of at least 30 lbs weight. Between the line and the bait is a leader about 30 centimetres long, which must be stiff for the jerks to make the bait shoot out toward the sides, and to lessen the risk of the bait getting caught up in the cast.

Baits

The baits fall into two general types: stickbaits and tailbaits. The latter have a spoon at the rear, which steers the bait downward during a jerk. The angle of the spoon can be changed for diving to different depths. Stickbaits are, in somewhat simplified terms, a stick with treble hooks and the most common jerkbait. In standard form, these baits go down to at most a metre below the water surface, since they can float. Hence, the technique is best in shallow waters, down to four

Jerkbait-fishing is one of the most reliable methods for big pike.

or five metres if the water is clear. This, in turn, means that jerkfishing is superb during early springtime, when the fish wander into shallow spawning areas, and during late autumn when they come in toward the shallow edges again.

If a standard jerkbait is weighted – by boring a hole in front of the midpoint, pushing in a fair amount of lead and gluing it shut – the bait can be made to run deeper. With a weight that keeps it suspended, neither sinking nor floating, it can be fished home very slowly, which is extremely effective when the water is really cold.

***Opposite top:** The baits are meant to imitate large, injured preyfish. This group of lures is represented here by a Fatso.*
***Opposite bottom:** Jerkbait-fishing gives the greatest rewards in terms of spectacular takes and afficient catches.*

Choosing the bait's colour

Many factors determine the effect of colour in artificial baits, so the rules for selecting colours cannot be strict. Besides, when the fish are on the take, colour often has no importance at all. But you should base a colour on the fish's natural prey. Some fresh waters are dominated by prey-fish such as crucian carp and rudd, which are imitated with gold and copper colours – while roach, bleak and smelt can be imitated with silvery colours. In clear flowing waters with trout and salmon, natural colours commonly do best.

Even the water's colour can influence the choice of colour. Frequently good in brownish waters are silver, copper and nickel, or strong and fluorescent colours. In dark, murky water, silvery and fluorescent colours are notably effective, and this applies equally to the cold months when the fish are much less active. Provocation is another key ingredient in selecting colours: you can choose one that provokes the fish to bite, such as a fluorescent colour.

The significance of colours is best understood by knowing which colours of light are absorbed in the water. In clear water, nearly all colours penetrate to a depth of 5 metres; below this, the red colours are absorbed while yellow, green and blue prevail. Spinning, however, is done mainly in shallower waters where all colours are visible.

Predatory fish in shallow waters often have bright colours. For example, a perch in clear shallow water has red fins and a yellowish body, whereas in murky deep water it has yellow or grey-white fins and light-grey scales. Thus, in shallow waters the choice of colour is important, but in deep water the challenge is rather to use lures that the fish can see and to present them in the right way.

Size and gait

Many fishermen are insecure when spinning, and arm themselves with numerous types of lures, until they find good ones. Then they gradually limit themselves to a handful of lures, whose gait and catching qualities they have confidence in. They know how their "favourites" fish at different depths, and the retrieval speeds and techniques – as well as colours – which are best in the water at hand.

Some general rules, though, exist for choosing the correct lure. First, a lure's weight should make it possible to fish effectively in the given water. If the fish are far out, the lure must

Left: The value of lure colours is often exaggerated, but in many waters the
colour can be as influential as the lure's shape, size and movements. As a rule,
in brownish and murky water (upper photo) strong colours should be used –
such as silver, copper, gold, flash and fluorescents. In clear water (lower
photo) natural and dark colours are recommended instead, such as silver –
alone or combined with blue or black – and zebra or "nature colours". One
must also, of course, take account of which preyfish occur in the given water,
at what depth the lure will work, and whether the sky is bright or dark.

be heavy enough for casting to them. If they are standing
deep, the weight of the lure should enable it to fish along the
bottom, throughout the retrieval distance.

Big fish are normally attracted by large lures, since they prefer taking a single mouthful to many small bites. Likewise, if
the water becomes murky or disturbed by wind and weather,
you should choose a larger lure with more flash or colour. The
worse the water gets, the less shy the predatory fish are.

The movements of artificial baits point to a further rule.
Salmon and trout, as well as bass and perch, are most tempted by lures that have a quick, enticing gait. On the other hand,
relatively slow movements draw predators such as pike,
pikeperch and musky.

Finally, one should keep in mind all the external factors
that affect the choice of lure: the wind, weather, season, air
pressure, the water's level and colour, its temperature and clarity, and the type of bottom – sandy or muddy, vegetated or
bare, flat or rolling. Lakes or waterways, and the times of day
you fish at – such as morning, evening, or in bright sunshine –
are further variables. In addition, of course, the choice will
depend on the fish's spawning, migrations, feeding habits,
and the preyfish in your water. These are factors you cannot
do much about, but must adapt to.

When spinning, however, a fisherman has full control over
certain essentials: how the lure is presented – at what depth
and retrieval speed – and its colour, gait and size. In sum,
adeptness at spinning does call for a fair share of experience.

The right lure in the right situation

Experienced fishermen know that faith in a particular lure can be more important than the lure
itself. This is undoubtedly because a believer in the
lure's superiority fishes with greater self-confidence
and presents it more attractively. Greater experience
also brings a better ability to choose baits that
attract fish in given situations, and to present them
in a manner realistic for the fish. However, this
depends on the fish being willing to bite.
Presenting the right bait correctly is thus not
enough: one has to fish at the right place and time
as well. Coaxing a scared, sluggish or sated fish
onto the hook is much harder than tricking an
active and hungry one...

Fishing in fresh waters
Pike

The pike (*Esox lucius*) is one of the biggest predators in fresh water, and a more popular quarry today than ever before. It inhabits lakes, pools, rivers and streams, ranging from northern Norway to Italy and far into Asia, as well as in much of the eastern and northeastern United States, Canada and Alaska. However, pike are not happy in Arctic, deep, cold lakes or high mountain waters. Like numerous other freshwater species, they tolerate a certain salt content. They can live in seas with salinity up to 0.7% and are therefore also common in, for example, large parts of the Baltic.

Pike have all the hallmarks of a good sportfish. Their way of life, appearance, and ability to grow heavy are fascinating to many sportfishermen. In Europe their weights exceed those in America. Pike of around 20 kilograms (44 pounds) are landed every year by Europeans, while the limits are 15-18 kg (33-40 lbs) in North America, although most places yield pike of up to 6-7 kg (13-15 lbs). This species also has some close relatives. The chain pickerel, weighing up to 1.5 kg (3.3 lbs), and two even smaller species, occur only in North America. Another instance is the muskellunge, and Asia boasts the Amur pike.

Spinning for pike

A hungry pike is not hard to get on the hook, but as a rule the fishing calls for an awareness of spinning methods and baits, and of the pike's holding places. In early spring, late autumn and winter, the water is cold and you have to retrieve slowly. Artificial lures should be worked across the bottom with many spin-stops, alternating slow and rapid retrieval. Between late spring and early autumn, the warmer water increases the fish's activity, so the retrieval must be livelier and still more varied.

Spinning for pike can be categorized by the depth of water involved. In shallow water, light spoons of thin sheet metal

Pike are a popular species of sportfish in numerous countries, mainly because this gluttonous predator can grow very large and is common in many waters. It can also offer exciting and spectacular fishing.

Vital facts

When the water warms up in spring, the pike pre-
pare to spawn. A female pike grows larger than
males, and is followed by one or more of them
during the mating. Her eggs hatch after 10-15 days
and the fry live on food such as small insects and
larvae. Once a few centimetres long, the young
pike begins to eat fish fry. It grows fastest in water
with plenty of preyfish whose sizes suit its success-
ive years of growth. The pike has a vigorous appetite
and prefers preyfish weighing 10-15% as much as it
does. If the preyfish are abundant, it usually eats a
big meal 1-2 times weekly, instead of constantly
chasing little fish. This manner of hunting character-
izes stocks of large pike, while small pike are in a
continuous state of growth and therefore feed more
often. Probably as a result, the pike is famous for
rising to bite in particular periods. It is also cannibalistic, and it eats a great deal besides fish – including
frogs, water voles, and young birds.

Pike hunt chiefly by using their sight, but have
well-developed senses of taste and smell – as is
shown by the ease of catching them with dead baitfish. They are most active in daylight, and studies
have revealed that they become almost totally inac-
tive in darkness.

Though normally staying at the bottom, pike are
sometimes found much higher up. Thus, it is not
quite true that pike are typical bottom-fish
dwelling among reeds and tree roots. They are
especially active in autumn and just after spawning. During these periods, too, they often occur in
the shallows. Summer brings them into deeper
water, for example at submerged edges and shoals.
But in cold climates, as in Scandinavia and Canada,
you can fish for big pike in shallow water throughout the summer.

are used. Small spinners of 7-12 grams are classic lures for pike, but light spinners with large spoons and a high gait are also very effective. Floating plugs are superb when spinning in shallow water. As soon as the water temperature rises, surface plugs start to pay off among reeds, water-lilies and other vegetation. Even the biggest surface plugs, such as the Suick, do excellently in shallows.

In wider lakes, pike move to deep water during the late spring. Once they go below 3-4 metres, however, heavier equipment is needed. Before the retrieval begins, the lures should be given time to sink to the bottom, since that is where the pike are lurking.

Heavy drags of 25-35 and sinking plugs are fine in deep water. As you retrieve, many pauses should be made, enabling the lure to stay at the bottom all the time. Fishing with weighted, floating plugs may also be effective. The line or leader is weighted according to the depth, the retrieval speed, and the plug's size and weight. Small plugs, of course, require less weighting than big ones.

Weight-forward spinners are the only type of spinner that works well for pike in deep water. This type is used down to 8-10 metres.

A pike's jaws are endowed with hundreds of teeth that can quickly shred the line, so it is always essential to use a steel leader when spinning. A leader 20-35 cm (8-14 in) long is perfect, but you can tie your own leaders with, for example, nylon line of 0.65-0.75 mm.

Pike fishing with natural bait

The practice of fishing with dead or live baitfish is widespread primarily in Great Britain and Central Europe, where this tradition has existed for ages. It is most effective in coloured and hard-fished waters, especially during the cold months and when the holding places of pike tend to be well-defined and familiar. Compared to the mobility of spinning, every form of

Left: When a pike is on the take, it seldom proves hard to tempt with a spinner, spoon or wobbler. Often, though, one must know where the pike are holding, and adapt one's spinning method accordingly.

Right: Among the most effective lures when spinning for pike is a wobbler (plug), whose movements and shape imitate the fish's natural prey quite well. A wobbler can also be fished at nearly all depths, and is thus able to trick deeply dwelling big pike onto the hook.

fishing with natural bait has a limited degree of water coverage – yet experience shows that large pike are often caught with baitfish.

The majority of live baitfish with lengths of 10-20 cm (4-8 in) can be used, such as roach, bleak and other whitefish. However, it is forbidden to use live baitfish in several countries, including Norway, Holland and Germany. Fishing with dead baitfish is usually done with roach and herring, but pieces of eel have also proved their worth.

There are two main ways of fishing with baitfish. One is float-fishing, with a fixed or sliding float, depending on the water depth. The baits can be presented either at the bottom or in free water. The other method is bottom-fishing with a fixed or sliding tackle, possibly combined with a sliding float.

Both live and dead baitfish are mounted with a treble hook in the tail. Many pike fishermen use two treble hooks for dead bait – one in the tail and one in the side. The hooks are placed with their tips pointing backward, since the pike normally take the prey crosswise and turn it in their jaws, then swallow it with the head forward. This fishing employs a steel leader 35-40 cm (14-16 in) long. In the case of dead baitfish, one often uses a bite indicator, and usually fishes with two rods at the same time. Treble hooks of sizes 4-10, depending on how big the preyfish are, serve ideally here. The best size for baitfish is 15-20 cm (6-8 in).

Spinning with dead baitfish is also enjoyed in some countries. Most simply, the baitfish is mounted with a treble hook in the upper and lower jaws, and another in the side. Then the baitfish is weighted with lead on the leader, and retrieved slowly or in jerks. Floats may also be used for simple spinning.

Ready-made tackle for spinning with baitfish is available as well. Such a tackle consists of two or three small treble hooks, a

Natural baits can be extremely rewarding in some types of water. But this fishing requires much greater knowledge of the fish's locations than does spinning with artificial lures. Perch and roach are common baitfish, and other small fish can also appeal to pike.

leaded head, and a loop which is run into the baitfish. In recent years an East European tackle, the Drakovitch, has won notable popularity for spinning with dead baitfish. It simplifies a type of tackle that has existed for decades in Central Europe. The retrieval is done in jerks near the bottom with repeated spin-stops.

Fighting and landing the fish

During the fight, an even and strong pressure is kept on the pike, and in shallow waters it does its best to leap. In many countries, fish are traditionally released to the water. For this purpose, a pike can be either beached or else landed with a large hand-net. But a net is unsuitable when you fish with big plugs, since the hooks easily catch in its meshes. A gaff is also commonly used in some countries, being carefully drawn into the lower jaw corner. Alternatively, the pike can be gripped beneath the gill with a leather or working glove. Small pike may be landed by taking a firm grip over the neck.

Small pike can be landed easily with a steady grip over the neck, but for larger ones a net or gaff should be used. An important point is to tire the pike out thoroughly before landing it, since otherwise it may shake itself off the hook. Once it is weary, it can be led into the net – which should then be in the water – and lifted.

Muskellunge

The musky (*Esox masquinongy*) is a relative of the pike that occurs in the northeastern United States and in southeastern Canada from Lake Abitibi down to Lake of the Woods. Farther south, it lives in the upper Mississippi and Ohio Rivers, in New York, Pennsylvania and Tennessee, North Carolina and Georgia, as well as in the St. Lawrence River and the Great Lakes. It can grow larger than pike – up to 25 kg (55 lbs). Excessive sportfishing for decades has decimated its stocks, and examples over 10 kg (22 lbs) are now rare. Yet specimens of 10-15 kg (22-33 lbs) are still caught every year in, for example, the St. Lawrence and its tributaries. While even so-called professional sportfishermen must devote several days to hooking a musky, it is considered by many to be the ultimate "pikefish".

Vital facts

The musky spawns in shallow water, preferably on a smooth bottom with tree roots and branches, at about the same temperature as for pike – but the spawning occurs at night. Afterward, the musky stays in shallow clear water, around vegetation banks, seldom at depths of more than 4-5 metres.

Occasionally these fish wander out to deeper water, where they are nearly impossible to catch. In rivers, they prefer the deep calm parts, and their most typical holding places are at inflows. They stay in the same areas during most of the summer, although the warmth in rivers often makes them migrate higher up.

Musky grow fast, and eat like gluttons in springtime. Late summer and especially autumn are regarded as best for musky fishing. The females become larger than the males, and the growth is most rapid in the northern latitudes of distribution. One musky of 69.7 lbs (31.6 kg) has been age-determined to 30 years. The fish's menu is identical to the pike's, as is its way of hunting.

Left: The musky, a close relative of the pike, occurs only in North America. It normally weighs 11-22 lbs (5-10 kg) and is caught chiefly in autumn, with artificial or natural baits.

Among other terms for this fish are muskalonge, lunge, blue pike and muskallunge. It is long and slender, somewhat paler than a pike, and has distinct wide vertical stripes. There are three subspecies within the musky's region of distribution. It is thought to have originally lived in salt water and migrated up the Mississippi – where the stocks were isolated due to the Ice Age, and from where it later spread out. Fossils show that it also existed in southern Europe during the Tertiary period.

Spinning for musky

Musky can be caught both by spinning and with natural bait on tackle, but spinning is the usual method. In general, rapid retrieval gives the best results. Large "bucktail" spinners, spinnerbaits and buzzbaits are designed for musky. This was originally also true of many of the surface plugs which are now used for pike.

Most big muskellunge are females, and are normally caught in September and October – often during the afternoon. Musky fishing demands a lot of patience. The fish is a loner and frequently needs a great number of casts to be tempted into taking. Pike may follow the bait once or twice before taking, but this behaviour is more typical of musky.

Right: A "freshwater crocodile" has taken the bait and tries desperately to get free of it during the fight's last phase.

Zander

The European pikeperch, or zander (*Stizostedion lucioperca*), is naturally distributed across Eastern Europe, Russia and southern Siberia. From there it has spread to western Europe and occurs from southern Scandinavia down to the northern parts of Italy and Spain. It has even been implanted in Great Britain, though not appreciated by English anglers. Zander also live in brackish water, and can be found throughout the Baltic.

A close relative is the Volga zander, in southeastern Europe as well as much of Russia and Siberia. In the United States and Canada are two others – the walleye and sauger.

This fish enjoys murky water, where it faces no competition from pike. It hunts smaller fish such as roach, bleak and perch. Wide waters are its preferred habitat, to depths of at least 4-5 metres.

Spinning for zander

Sight, smell and hearing are all used by zander when they hunt. But the spinning technique used for pike has no impact on these fish, since they cannot swim as fast or see as well. The key to zander fishing is slow retrieval with good bottom contact and, ideally, bait that "jabs" the bottom – thus relying on the fish's hearing and sight.

Probably one of the best types of artificial lures for zander is the jig. Its special body and upturned hook also make it easy to fish just over the bottom.

A jerky retrieval creates sounds that attract pikeperch. Jigs with silicone bodies are extremely effective. The combination of a jig with fish strips is arousing, too, as it activates the zander's sense of smell. Many scent-impregnated rubber bodies work superbly on zander. In all seasons and water temperatures, you should retrieve slowly and jerkily, though a bit faster during the hot months. A jig performs as spectacularly in still waters as in flowing waters, where the zander prefer deep channels with stones and considerable current.

Weight-forward spinners are well suited to spinning for zander. They not only give better bottom contact, but can be

Pikeperch are active in darkness, and spend most of their time at the bottom in deep water. They should be fished by retrieving slowly and trying to keep in contact with the bottom.

retrieved in jerks and continue to rotate as they sink. Moreover, the spinner head generates clear sounds when it hits the bottom.

Spinning with a plug – which may be a "deep-going" type with a rattle and a long bill – is unbeatable for zander. The rattle makes sounds that attract the fish while the deep-diving plug's spoon jabs the bottom. It was once commonly believed that zander are partial to small preyfish, and thus also small

baits, but with experience they are found to gobble even big plugs of up to 20 cm (8 in).

No matter what type of artificial bait you use, false bites are frequent, and time alone can teach you to distinguish "bottom contact" from a zander's cautious nibble. Hence it is important to use needle-sharp hooks and, if possible, replace the treble hook with a thinner one – especially in water with lots of little zander.

Vital facts

Zander spawn from late March until the beginning or middle of April, at a higher temperature than for pike. The sticky eggs are laid on branches and stones in shallow water. River mouths, too, are favourite spawning places. After a few weeks the spawning ends, when the temperature reaches 15-16° C (59-61° F). But windy weather can quickly silt up the eggs and the spawning bottoms. This is one reason why zander stocks are classified according to good and bad years.

Soon after hatching, young zander eat water-fleas and plankton. Next they adopt a menu of fish fry and small fish. Similarly to pike, they are also cannibalistic.

The zander has a special way of hunting, which is shown by its shape and body structure. Being less slender than the pike, it cannot swim fast. Yet its night vision is excellent, and it has large eyes that shine like reflectors in a lamp's light. It is built to live on the bottom, where it can follow prey for long distances. The prey is attacked from behind. Zander in general are active fish in cloudy weather and at night.

During the summer, zander move out to the shoals and edges in deep water. At evening and night, they return to hunt in shallow water or higher levels. Towards morning when it gets light, they swim back to the depths. These daily migrations also occur in autumn. During that season and in winter, they often run up rivers and streams. Zander always prefer hard bottoms – stone, sand, cliffs and banks. Small ones are quite sociable and frequently form little schools to stay in limited areas. Large zander are usually solitary.

It is typical for a stock of zander that the fishing is good for some years but then deteriorates. Such variations are presumably due to the supply of prey-fish. Many waters contain zander of 1-3 kg (2.2-6.6 lbs) and bigger ones only exceptionally. In other waters, there can be a few years of fine fishing for medium or large zander, whereupon the fish die out – to revive a few years later. Examples of 1-2.5 kg are the rule, while weights of 5-8 kg (11-18 lbs) are rare and the maximum is 12-14 kg (26-31 lbs).

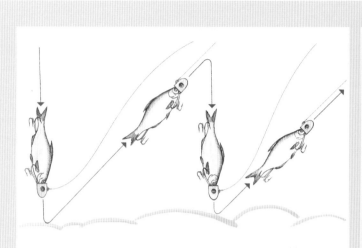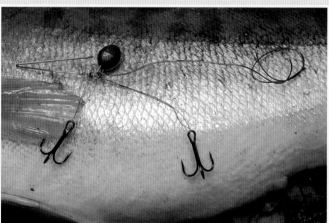

When fishing with natural bait, the weighted baitfish is fished in with repeated spin-stops and good bottom contact. The upper picture shows a so-called Drakovitch rig, with a shackle that is run into the baitfish's belly.

Keep in mind that zander are most active by dark – whether in the morning, evening, night, or during cloudy and windy days. On the whole, low-pressure weather is best. On bright days the fish must be sought in deep water. Particularly during winter and just before it ices up, shallow water can yield zander. What the species may lack in fighting spirit – compared for example to pike and trout – it definitely outweighs with its unpredictable behaviour, which has thrilled sportfishermen down the centuries. Besides, it is a marvelous food fish.

Zander fishing with natural bait

The zander's manner of using its senses make it a true challenge to catch with natural baitfish. It bites somewhat hesitantly and may be shy. A sliding tackle is therefore best used. This allows the fish to swim away with the bait and feel no resistance from the sinker. You can also combine sliding tackle with a sliding float.

An electronic bite indicator is employed when you have fish strips, fillets, or dead baitfish on the hook. A steel leader is not necessary, but this or some other strong leader material is worth using, since the fishing often takes place in waters that also contain pike. A nylon leader of 0.35-0.40 mm is quite adequate, unless you fish in areas with roots, stones and other

obstacles that the fish can exploit.

When fishing with live baitfish, the treble hook is inserted in the back or tail, or between the dorsal and tail fins. With dead baitfish or fish strips, though, it is stuck in the tail root or the thin part of the strip. Use hooks of size 6-10 according to the bait's size. Baitfish of 12-16 cm (4.5-6.5 in) are fine for zander.

All fishing with natural bait is done on, or just over, the bottom. During the night, zander move upward in the water, so at a lake's shoals and edges it is occasionally best to fish a couple of metres above the bottom.

Opposite left: The pikeperch is not famous for being a great fighter, but it is an excellent foodfish. Since it can be difficult to hook, sharp and slender hooks are often necessary.

Opposite right: Being relatively shy, a pikeperch frequently takes the bait with careful hesitation. Gliding tackle is thus usually best for catching it, either at the bottom or some metres up.

Perch

The perch (*Perca fluviatilis*) occurs all over Europe, Asia and North America, except in the Arctic regions and in clear, cold mountain lakes. It also enjoys brackish water and is common along the Baltic coasts. There are perch in the smallest meres as well as the biggest lakes and rivers. This fish is easily recognized by the black stripes over its back, and its red or yellow fins. Its colours tend to be strongest in clear water. It weighs from a few tenths of a kilogram up to 2-3 kg (4.4-6.6 lbs).

Spinning for perch

Because of their capricious inclination to take bait, perch provide exciting experiences for sportfishermen. One day they may attack whatever moves, and the next day you may try everything in the bait-box with no results. If a perch follows a spoon, spinner, jig or plug without biting, this is a sign of unwillingness. A varied retrieval with many spin-stops and tugs is then important. Impulsive and unusual methods of

Vital facts

Perch spawn in shallow water during early spring, and then move to deeper water. While the perch in shallow lakes and rivers pursue a vagabond life, big lakes contain both pelagic perch that hunt in deep water, and typical shallow-water perch that occur near the shores almost all year round.

Being a distinctively predatory fish, the perch prefers clear water – but in murky water its spawning opportunities are often better, and neither its eggs nor young are as easily noticed by other fish. Thus coloured waters tend to have abundant stocks of small perch.

This is a sociable fish and usually lives in schools of varying size. They gather at deep edges, shoals, in deep parts of streams, at boat piers or bridge pillars. A school also gives good protection against higher predators.

retrieval are frequently essential to attract such perch. Even a particular movement may be what triggers their reflex – or a certain colour of bait, since perch have excellent colour vision. Once the first perch has taken bait, it commonly starts a chain reaction and others do so as well.

Perch are not confined to the bottom: often they occur 2-3 metres up. During the summer, they may hunt small fish in the surface, and their presence in big lakes is often revealed by diving gulls. It is therefore wise to search a body of water in different ways, for example at the bottom, just above it, in the middle layer and at the surface.

However wild and greedy the perch is when biting, it can be sly and unreachable when, for instance, the weather makes it unwilling. There are many indications that its mood is influenced by the air pressure. A stable low or high pressure is normally good for the fishing, yet a rapidly falling or rising pressure may lead perch virtually to stop hunting. Still, some sportfishermen have quite the opposite impression about how air pressure affects the fishing.

Spinning for perch can be pursued with almost all types of artificial lures, but certain types do work better than others. Spinners and small spoons are traditionally used in shallow waters, although fishing with a jig is usually best. In deep waters, great success is often achieved with a heavier jig, a lead-headed spinner, or deep-going sinking plugs.

Using a dropper, a little fly or micro-jig, above the lure is a fine trick to play on perch. Their innate curiosity, together with envy of the little prize, can provoke a bite. Slow, jerky retrieval is especially worthwhile with dropper flies, which can also be baited with worms, larvae, or a piece of fish skin. Moreover, perch love strong or contrasting colours such as red/black, orange/yellow and white/red. Marked "eyes" on a jig may yield further attraction.

Opposite: Characteristic of a perch are its black transverse stripes from the back down toward the abdomen, and red or orange-yellow fins. The clearer the water is, the stronger the colours tend to be.

Bass

The American bass may well be the most popular sportfish in the world. There are six species and four subspecies of American black bass, but in practice they are divided into smallmouth bass (*Micropterus dolomieu*), weighing up to 4 kg (8.8 lbs), and largemouth bass (*Micropterus salmoides*) which can weigh nearly 10 kg (22 lbs). These have different distributions. Smallmouth bass originally lived in the northeastern United States and southeastern Canada, and have not spread as far as largemouth bass. The latter first inhabited the eastern USA, from the Great Lakes to Florida and the prairies, but has spread by implantation and now occurs in all the western states. It has also been quite successfully implanted in Mexico and Central America, as in Guatemala and Costa Rica. The same was done in Cuba as early as 1915, and it exists in Hawaii. Largemouth bass even reached Brazil in 1926, and can be found in 16 African countries such as Morocco and South Africa.

In 1879 an English biologist brought the bass to Europe, and it was implanted in many countries – including Hungary, Austria, Switzerland and Russia – but died out. Today there are small stocks in the southern parts of Germany and France, although it is more widespread in Italy and Spain. At most places in Europe it weighs hardly over 2 kg (4.4 lbs), but Spain has the best bass waters and yields specimens up to 5 kg (11 lbs).

In the USA, bass have spread along with people, being regarded as a good "reserve fish" to keep on farms. All canals, lakes, rivers, reservoirs and small ponds now contain bass. These fish tolerate high temperature, multiply easily and grow fast. Their inability to live in many countries is due to their need of warm water at 20° C (68° F) during May and June, when they spawn. On the other hand, they survive in water up to 30° C (86° F). Yet they cannot take murky or muddy waters, and have thus done poorly in many African countries, whose rivers are often turbid.

Bass are extremely popular sportfish, notably in the USA. They occur in both deep and shallow waters, but are typical warm-water fish, so one usually finds them in the water areas with highest temperature.

Vital facts

After the spawning, which takes place in shallow water, fishermen begin to spin for bass. However, the fishing depends on the weather and improves as it gets warmer. Bass have a broad diet – from small worms and insects to fish fry, small fish, mice and frogs. They often behave sociably and may move in little schools, groups or "packs", but are also found individually.

As a rule, bass alternate between deep and shallow water but do not go very far. They presumably maintain territories and spend most of the time there at the bottom. When encountered in shallow water, they stay near vegetation – reeds, lilies, trees, and whatever else can provide shade or protection, as well as edible small fish.

Bass fishing is not difficult once you find the quarry. This is the real problem, besides deciding the right type of artificial bait. At the start of the season, the bass are in shallow water where the temperature is highest, and as it approaches 20-21° C (68-70° F) your chances improve. Later in the season, when the water gets too warm, the bass move to deeper water and must be sought at the bottom – very seldom in the middle layer. While they linger among plants and stones in shallow water, deep water finds them at reefs, edges and shoals, as preyfish gather there too. In the morning and evening, the bass return to shallow water along the shores – and notably in vegetated waters, fishing in the morning is best of all. Towards autumn and winter, the bass are again wherever the temperature is highest.

Spinning for bass

Bass fishing is not easy in deep water, and the finest experiences are obtained in shallows that help you to hook the fish. A bass can see extremely well, which makes the bait's colour important, but it is still more essential to retrieve slowly at depth along the bottom. However, even if this applies to four out of five fishing trips, the fifth may show that a rapid retrieval is better. Generally, you should retrieve near the bottom, although there are rare occasions when bass can actually be caught at the surface – for example during the morning and evening. Of course, surface fishing for bass is more common in shallow clear lakes, ponds and rivers.

Fishing with a jig is the oldest and most widespread method of spinning for bass. But it requires the fisherman to have con-trol over the bait's movements, since the jig itself shows little life during a uniform retrieval with no variations. Proper jig fishing involves casting out, letting the jig sink, and then spinning it in with short tugs – slowly or with rapid changes of movement.

The fishing is easy over smooth bottoms, but it becomes much harder in areas that are rolling, vegetated, or full of trees and roots. Particularly for smallmouth bass, it is necessary to fish at the bottom, because this species tends to stay on bottoms with stones and cliffs. Largemouth bass are more readily caught somewhat above the bottom, as they are drawn to plants and other sources of shade.

When fishing from a boat in shallow water, you can benefit by using spinnerbait. This is retrieved in the surface at first and then allowed to sink, so as to attract the attention of bass.

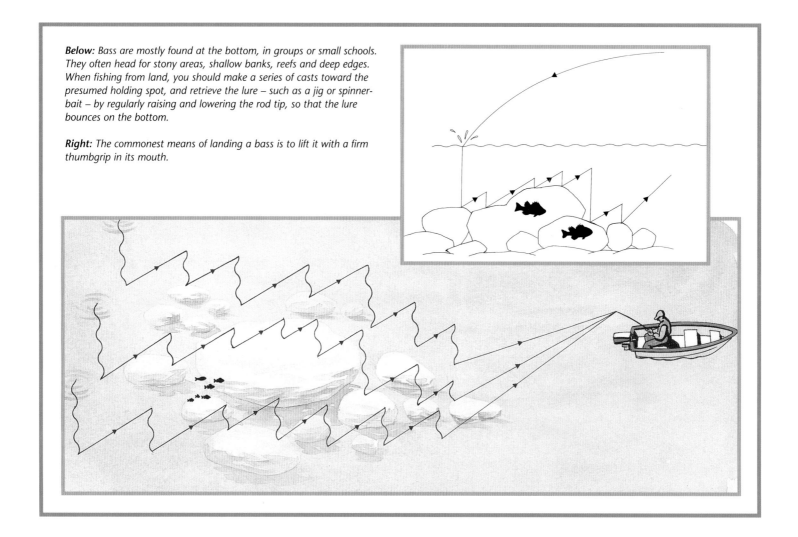

Below: Bass are mostly found at the bottom, in groups or small schools. They often head for stony areas, shallow banks, reefs and deep edges. When fishing from land, you should make a series of casts toward the presumed holding spot, and retrieve the lure – such as a jig or spinner-bait – by regularly raising and lowering the rod tip, so that the lure bounces on the bottom.

Right: The commonest means of landing a bass is to lift it with a firm thumbgrip in its mouth.

Spoons, spinners, and all sorts of plugs – surface types, sinking and floating – are excellent both in shallow water and out to several metres of depth. In deeper water, deep-diving plugs and weight-forward spinners are recommended. There is no doubt, however, that most sportfishermen find greater excitement in fishing the shallows with surface plugs, as well as with plastic worms. These long silicone creatures are mounted on a hook, forming a so-called Texas rig, which comes in different versions.

As in so many other kinds of sportfishing, one should fish for bass with thin lines and small baits on a bright day in clear water. Warm days and periods call for concentration on the morning hours, starting to fish before it gets light. A rippled surface is often more advantageous than mirror-smooth water. You should also keep quiet and avoid making noise in a boat or with its engine

Bass fishing with natural bait

If the fishing is slack, natural baits are frequently best – such as small live fish, lampreys, bee larvae, grasshoppers, salamander, crustaceans, leeches and worms. All kinds of natural bait for bass should be set on a single hook, so that they look more lively. Use as little weighting as possible – and as small a float as possible, if you prefer to fish with a float. Once the bait sinks after the cast, be sure that the bass can easily pull out line when it bites, and then make your strike.

Right: Many sportfishermen consider plastic worms to be a thrilling way of catching bass. No matter whether you use a Texas or Carolina rig, the fish can hardly resist the long silicon worm on it – as this largemouth bass learned.

Far right: Just as for many other species, the "golden hours" of morning and evening are generally best for bass.

Bluegill

The bluegill (*Lepomis macrochirus*) is a popular "public fish" in the United States. Its colours differ widely between waters, but it often has 6-8 stripes across its back and sides, which may be yellowish or dark blue. It seldom weighs more than 1 kg (2.2 lbs), although some are nearly twice as heavy. Bluegill were originally distributed from Minnesota down to the Great Lakes, southward to Georgia and westward to Arkansas. Today the species is implanted in numerous small ponds in almost every state.

Spinning for bluegill

Catching a bluegill is commonly the first fishing experience for a child, and the pleasure of it may last a lifetime. This is an entertaining, wild and bite-crazy fish, taking the tiniest of artificial lures – spinners, spoons, and primarily jigs. As a rule, one succeeds best with a slow, varied retrieval. But you may well have to try different types of bait before you find just the one that triggers the fish's reflex. At times, the very first cast attracts a bite – and next a whole school can dissolve as soon as the bait hits the water. In any case, wherever the first bluegill is caught, more of them are likely to be available. An imaginative retrieval with light equipment can yield many fine rewards.

Vital facts

Bluegill live in clear, small ponds and lakes with vegetation, overhanging and fallen trees, but can also be found in city environments such as parks. The fish spawn in May and, for a few days, the fry are protected by the male. They grow slowly, often resulting in overpopulation of the water. Their diet consists of larvae, water insects, crustaceans, and occasionally small fish or fry. Bluegill tend to occur in rather shallow water, although big ones are sometimes caught in deeper areas. They swim in dispersed schools of no great size.

Panfish is a collective name for bluegill, crappie, perch and "white perch". Here we see a bluegill, which not only tastes fine but is also an enjoyable sportfish, taking either artificial or natural baits.

Bluegill fishing with natural bait

Perhaps the most familiar way of catching bluegill today is with a float, a single leader, a couple of lead shot, and a worm on a small hook. Yet combinations of artificial and natural baits are frequently better, such as small jigs baited with mealworm, earthworm or larvae.

sides. They often weigh up to 1 kg (2.2 lbs) and the record exceeds 2 kg. Both species are just as generous and willing to bite as the bluefish.

Spinning for crappies

Crappies also resemble bluegill in being a great challenge to catch with ultra-light spinning gear. The smallest spinners, spoons and plugs are very effective, but jigs are probably the best choice, since the fish often circulate in overgrown waters and in places with vegetation, branches and rough bottoms. The fish stay at the bottom regardless of whether it is in a sunny, shallow cove or in deep water.

Crappie fishing with natural bait

These fish eagerly take natural bait. A single float with a leader, and a hook baited with a worm or a small fish, are convenient and profitable. As in fishing for bluegill, you can also use artificial lures – chiefly jigs that are baited with a fish strip, a whole little fish, worms, larvae or some other accessible bait. Normally baited jigs are used, but the fish then needs a bit more time to swallow the bait before you strike. Crappies have a large mouth and are tired out by keeping an even pressure on the line with no jerks.

Vital facts

Crappies thrive in lakes, ponds, and slow-flowing rivers or streams throughout the USA. Black crappie is most common in the northern states, while the white species occurs in the south. They enjoy clear water with vegetation and overhanging trees – mainly willows – where shade and protection are provided by rich plant life. Enthusiastic crappie fishermen thus often build shelters in the water, for example with mats made of reeds or branches.

The fish can be caught by either day or night, from some time after spawning until the autumn. Dusk, however, is regarded as the best hour. This is a popular quarry for ice-fishing, too. Like bluegill, crappies can overpopulate the water. They live on insects, worms, crustaceans, fry and small fish.

Crappie

Here is another extremely popular fish, which – along with bluegill, perch and "white perch" – is known as panfish, since all of them are wonderful to eat. The two species are black crappie (*Pomoxis nigromaculatus*), which has black patches spread over its sides, and white crappie (*Pomoxis annularis*) whose patches are merged into stripes across its back and

Catfish

A catfish is easily recognized by its flat head, which comprises 20% of the body – and by its "beard" of barbels, or feelers, which are a tenth as long as the body. Catfish occur on every continent, and there are hundreds of species in the world. Apart from the sturgeon, and carp species in the Amazon and eastern Asia, catfish are among the biggest of all fish in fresh waters. The European wels (*Siluris glanis*) grows largest, to over 200 kg (440 lbs), followed by other species in the Amazon and Mekong Rivers, while the smallest catfish in the group Silurodei are only a few centimetres long.

A further example is the electric catfish, *Malapterus electricus*, which can generate up to 350 volts. In the United States are several species, such as the flathead and the blue catfish, weighing as much as 25-50 kg (55-110 lbs). Channel catfish are also common, but they seldom weigh more than 8-9 kg (18-20 lbs).

The wels originally lived in Central and Eastern Europe as well as in Asia. It has spread to, and been implanted in, many countries – and today it inhabits a number of rivers in France, Italy, Spain and Germany. The northern limit of its distribution runs through southern Sweden and Finland and the Baltic.

Spinning for catfish

One can scarcely believe that catfish, with their relatively poor eyesight and dependence on dusk or murky water for much activity, will take a plug or spoon – but the fact is that they do. They are intrigued by preyfish that appear sick or move oddly, and this is a basic feature of spinning. Artificial baits should be brought in with jerks and, at the same time, hit the bottom. Two types of lure are most suited to such retrieval, plugs and large jigs, even though spoons and spinners can also trick catfish.

The colours are not very important when spinning, but strongly coloured or fluorescent plugs have proved effective. The plugs should be retrieved with regular impacts on the bottom. Large jigs, perhaps combined with fish strips, or whole

Catfish can be very big and are then eager for large prey, so they are usually caught with natural baits – especially fish weighing up to about 3.5 lbs (1.5 kg).

Vital facts

These fish are typically adapted to warm water and become most active in summertime. They spawn in shallow water when the temperature is at least 20° C (68° F). Their eggs are laid on branches, roots and plant remains. The fry grow rather fast, are 30-40 cm (12-16 in) long after two years, and measure 50-80 cm (20-32 in) after 3-4 years.

To begin with, the young eat mostly larvae, worms and fish fry. Soon they are big enough to consume water voles, frogs and the like. Catfish are also cannibalistic, but their greediness is debatable. They eat less in comparison to their weight than, for example, pike do – for catfish are not as active. It is known from fish farms that a catfish must eat 6-7 kg (13-15 lbs) of fish for every kilogram of weight it gains.

When the catfish attains a certain size, it occupies a territory and forms a stock there. Catfish are found in lakes, but rarely in very deep water. They occupy the calm parts of rivers and streams, although seldom the deepest holes. Avoiding currents, they are drawn to areas with fallen or overhanging trees that offer shade and shelter. Tributaries from other rivers are also attractive holding places.

While catfish can be caught by day, they are quite active at night. Traditionally good times for fishing are the evening, night and dawn. Their activity is notably dependent on the temperature, and increases primarily when it gets warmer, whereas less warmth can make them almost completely stop biting. Thunderstorms with rain and a rising level of unclear water, too, can heighten their activity. Then they enter shallow waters to feed – but with a sinking level of clearer water, they lapse into inactivity. Catfish are preferably caught with live or naturally dead bait, and spinning for them has become more frequent in recent years.

fish on jig bodies, are superb as well. Moreover, whole fish on a tackle like the Drakovitch have become popular in spinning.

Catfish do not have "dangerous" teeth, so a leader of 0.50-0.70 mm is sufficient for spinning – as resistance to bottom stones and other obstacles, rather than to the fish's teeth. Often a catfish follows the lure and misses a few bites before it is hooked. You should cast repeatedly over a place where catfish are thought to be, since they are attracted by the lure's impact on the surface and its gait along the bottom. This fishing, of course, calls for strong spinning equipment and a reel that holds lots of thick line, such as 0.40-0.60 mm.

Catching catfish with natural bait

Natural baits are demonstrably effective on a night-hunter like the catfish, and are used by almost everyone who fishes for it. The bait may be dead or live fish, fillets or halves of fish, liver, earthworm snippets, leeches, and meat from mammals – even live or dead frogs, in countries where this bait is permitted. Among the classic types of bait are hen intestines and innards. Baitfish can weigh 100-500 grams, according to the size of fish you are after.

Bottom fishing with a sliding float and sliding tackle is the commonest method. At night, a bite indicator is used. When fishing from a boat, paternoster tackle is a standard accessory.

Many holding places of catfish are overgrown with vegetation, branches, roots and diverse hindrances. One fishes with a sliding float and fixed tackle, possibly of the paternoster type, and ideally somewhat above the bottom in order to avoid obstacles. Small catfish, in particular, often go higher over the bottom to take baitfish, and can thus be caught in the surface as well.

Observations show that catfish move away from their holding places twice each day – just before sunrise, and just before sunset – to hunt for food. Therefore, many fishermen concen-trate on these times, unless they are familiar with a holding place and can serve the bait exactly on or near it.

The equipment must be strong, especially at places with plenty of obstacles. Frequent use is made of line up to 0.65 mm, on multiplier or spinning reels. A very strong, metre-long leader of nylon, steel wire, or kevlar may be needed to resist branches, roots and stones.

There is also a Hungarian attractor, the "kuttjer". It consists of a short cane with a handle and a little flat head, as big as a large coin. Used chiefly when fishing from a boat, it is swung down into the water with a regular rhythm, every 1.5-2 seconds. Its sound resembles the pop of a champagne cork, and brings up catfish to bite. This device has become common in many countries, on both drifting and anchored boats.

Striking, fighting and landing the fish

When spinning, you must give a strike as soon as you feel a catfish taking, or spitting out, an artificial lure. But if fishing with natural bait, you should delay the strike a few seconds. Since the catfish's mouth is hard, the strike must be stiff – and it may have to be repeated, so that you know the hook is driven in. Catfish are in the habit of immediately, after the strike, heading back to their shelter among fallen trees or branches.

The fish should be held strongly, as it is very tough and persistent. During the fight, it often stays at the same place and can be difficult to get moving. You may succeed in making it swim by throwing stones at the place or otherwise frightening it with sounds.

An inexperienced fisherman can land a catfish with a large net, or a gaff in the middle of its lower jaw. The expert frequently uses a working glove to grip its lower jaw, with the thumb in its mouth. But a big fish requires extra manpower, for two hands are often necessary – one around the jaw and one in the gill.

Above: A hefty catfish has been landed after a long, tough struggle. Specimens of this size can scarcely be landed by oneself, and at least two men are needed here.

Left: A "kuttjer" in action. This attractor is slammed repeatedly on the water, and its sounds apparently stimulate catfish to bite.

Trout

The trout (*Salmo trutta*) has demonstrated great adaptability as a species. It occurs in clear, oxygen-rich waters, streams, mountain brooks and lakes, where several forms of it have evolved. In biological terms, the brown trout (*Salmo trutta fario*), the lake-run trout (*S. t. lacustris*), and the sea trout (*S. t. trutta*) belong to the same species. In many waters, all three of these develop from the same fish – depending on whether the offspring stay in flowing water, move into lakes, or migrate to the sea. They acquire different behaviour and colouring, but only a test of their scales can prove which is which.

Brown trout and lake-run trout were originally distributed in Europe – from the Mediterranean to northern Norway and Iceland, westward to the British Isles, and eastward far into Siberia. Trout were introduced to the eastern United States in 1883, then to New Zealand and other continents, such as South America, Africa and parts of Asia. However, these trout are not as tolerant of water temperatures as rainbow trout are. The ones implanted around the world derive from Loch Leven in Scotland, a lake north of Edinburgh that was once famous for its healthy, fast-growing stock of trout.

The size of brown trout varies widely according to their food supply. In European waterways, specimens of 2-3 kg (4.4-6.6 lbs) are unusual, while such weights are common in, for example, New Zealand. The maximum in flowing waters is 10 kg (22 lbs), but anything around 0.5-1 kg (1.1-2.2 lbs) is considered a fine brown trout.

Spinning for trout

The brown trout's manner of life differs between mountain rivers or brooks and the lowlands, whose nutritious, clear, oxygenated streams can make the fish quite selective about food. In flowing waters, the usual method is downstream fishing with spinners, spoons or small plugs. One then searches holding places – holes, furrows, banks of vegetation and so on. In a large waterway, you cast downstream toward the opposite bank, let the bait swing into the current, and retrieve it. Thus you can carry the search metre by metre downstream.

The trout – which, in flowing waters, is a typically territorial fish – lives mainly on insects, but increasingly adopts a fish diet as it grows. Thus it becomes ever easier to fool with spoons, spinners and plugs.

Vital facts

Trout in the northern hemisphere spawn from October until December. The fry become territorial, and this trait is kept throughout their lives in flowing waters. Trout have diverse periods of activity, determined mainly by the supply of insects. Brown trout are active primarily in the morning, evening, and briefly at midday.

Trout consume insects, larvae, worms and fish fry. They usually also develop cannibalistic tendencies. In waterways, about 90% of their food comprises insects that drift with the current, and 10% of surface insects. When hunting, they use their eyesight and, as shown by numerous studies, their lateral line organ.

The holding places of trout are those that enable them to spend as little energy as possible in resisting the current, and where they can find plenty of food – at current edges, shorelines and holes. Brown trout often choose shady places, unlike rainbow trout which happily live in free water.

Trout also live in lakes of all sizes. In a small lake, they cruise about and frequently enter the shore zone. Here they live chiefly on insects, crustaceans, larvae and worms, as well as fish fry. Vegetated areas, promontories, shallows, and stream outlets attract them most. During the summer, they move out to deep water, but often approach land in the morning and evening. While the brown trout in flowing waters can be hard to catch, the fish in lakes are more willing to bite. Consequently, trout have been implanted in many lakes known as "put-and-take" waters, where the sport's quality is determined by the stock and the fishing pressure. In large lakes with inflows that allow the fish to spawn, lake-run stocks with big fish develop. Various European lakes contain lake-run trout, which are either shiny with black spots or bronze-yellow.

A spinner works very well in flowing waters, as it runs smoothly in the current and is easy to guide by moving the rod up, down or sideways.

Insert: *A hooked trout often exposes itself at the surface by leaping and splashing. This habit obviously makes the fishing more fun, since you can see the fish during most of the fight.*

The fish in flowing waters are often shy and see the fisherman at a great distance. It is therefore wise to fish cautiously and throw no shadows on the surface – in other words, make oneself "as little as possible". When fishing downstream, the bait comes from behind and the trout see it for only a moment. They probably do not aim very well at a lure and, hence, often miss the bite, or else follow it and become frightened.

Upstream fishing, which reaches beyond the fish, requires better contact with the lures. These should work in a lively fashion and are retrieved a bit faster than the current speed. The advantage is that the trout sees the lure soon, can "time" its bite, and is usually hooked securely. But upstream fishing is much harder than downstream fishing, because the current keeps the lure working.

A spinner is the best type of bait in flowing water. Its blade's rotation creates a high gait, while the spinner maintains a good "grip" in the water. If you lower the rod, or retrieve more slowly, the spinner goes deeper. When you lift the rod or slightly speed up the retrieval, the spinner will rise in the water. It can be steered in the right path at holding places by moving the rod sideways.

Spoons can also be used in flowing water, though they do not "grip" the water as well as spinners do. A spoon is therefore usually led away from the current – or up toward the surface.

Floating plugs are excellent for fishing in shallow currents. They cannot be cast so far, but you can let them follow the current to within a couple of metres from the holding place and then retrieve. A floating plug may also be weighted, a short distance up on the line. In deeper waterways with relatively strong currents, sinking plugs are used.

Jigs are less common for trout fishing in flowing waters. Yet a jig is easy to cast, sinks rapidly, and is suited especially to fishing in current furrows and deep holes.

The trout in flowing waters are both shy and fastidious. It is not unusual for flyfishing on a popular waterway to catch more trout than spinning does. However, spinning with flies is quite feasible. You weight the line 60-80 cm (24-32 in) up, for example with lead shot, and use a trout fly with a single or double hook – or a small tube fly. The fly can swing in the current, or be retrieved like a spinner.

Trout have good colour vision. The rules for bait colour exist to be broken, of course – but in general one uses silver, nickel, yellow, and fluorescent colours in murky water, high water levels, darkness, and strong winds with surface waves. In clear water, low levels, and bright weather, it is best to try subdued colours and copper, but also dark hues and black.

In lakes or put-and-take waters, the same types of bait are employed, and spoons may be equally profitable. A casting Buldo together with a fly is effective in lakes, too. The Buldo can be attached in two basic ways – sliding and fixed. In the first case, the stopper consists of a swivel, to which is tied a leader

length of 1.2-3.5 metres (4-12 feet) depending, among other things, on the depth and on how shy the trout are. When the fish takes the fly, it can pull line without feeling resistance from the bubble. In the second case, favoured by many sportfishermen, the casting bubble and a quick strike are combined to hook the fish well.

Trout fishing with natural bait

In small flowing waters, no bait is more effective for trout than a drifting worm on an unweighted line. The worm is fished either upstream or downstream, and the current brings it down toward the trout. In wider or deeper waters, the worm tackle can be weighted with lead shot slightly up on the line.

But the simplest method is to fish with a float and a fairly long leader that is weighted according to the current and

When spinning in flowing water, it is normally best to cast the lure obliquely upstream. Once the lure has sunk, it is retrieved with a taut line along the bottom, and should more or less flutter along. If the current is weak, you may need to liven the lure by tugging with the rod tip, while retrieving slowly to make it bounce along the bottom.

Trout should be played with even pressure and relatively light force on the drag, so that the fish is not prevented from pulling line off the reel if it rushes.

depth. The hook is baited with a worm. The float then drifts with the current while you walk downstream after it or "trot" out line. A pull on the float shows that the trout is biting, but only when it disappears under the surface do you strike.

Substantial waterways are often fished with a tackle that may have a three-way swivel, but using a leader of 80-120 cm (32-48 in) and a sinker on its end. Again the hook is baited with a worm. This tackle is cast obliquely downstream and swings in toward – or over – a holding place, so that you maintain bottom contact.

In a lake, there are two means of fishing with natural bait: the simple tackle with a float – fixed or sliding, depending on the depth – or using a casting bubble and worms, which is retrieved. Both methods are extremely effective in most waters.

Although worms are the classic bait, one can very well fish with larvae, insects, crustaceans, small fish, or other natural baits. During late summer and autumn, or early in spring, waterways can also be fished – where this is allowed – with salmon eggs or the roe of trout and salmon. Eggs and roe are fished with or without a float, or else on bottom tackle which moves in the current.

Fighting the fish

The leaps of trout are well known to all sportfishermen. Yet a trout goes wild only if your drag is set too hard. So you have to follow the strike with an even pressure, letting the fish pull out line if it wants. Then it is landed with a net, or slid up on land if the shore is smooth.

Sea trout

While the sea trout (*Salmo trutta trutta*) is biologically the same species as brown trout, it is anadromous – migrating between marine and fresh waters, swimming up the river where it was born just as salmon do. Originally sea trout were distributed in northern Europe. The stocks now in other parts of the world derive from implanted brown trout, which in some places have formed anadromous stocks – as in New Zealand, Argentina and the Falklands. In eastern North America, a smaller stock of sea trout inhabits, for example, Newfoundland, Nova Scotia, Maine, New York and Connecticut. A true stock of sea trout was first introduced to North America in 1958.

In Europe, sea trout are common in the British Isles, Iceland, the Faeroes, Norway, Sweden, Denmark, Finland, the Baltic region and Poland. There is also a small stock in northern Germany and northern France. Those in the Baltic Sea are notable for rapid growth, and the Mörrum and Emån are well-known streams with large and vigorous sea trout.

Different strains of sea trout vary in their development. At most places, they seldom weigh over 2-3 kg (4.4-6.6 lbs). Large specimens occur in only a few Norwegian rivers, the Swedish Baltic rivers, Danish streams, and some rivers in Poland, the Baltic states and Finland, where they may weigh up to 10-14 kg (22-31 lbs) although the rule is 3-6 kg (6.6-13.2 lbs).

Spinning for sea trout

The methods of fishing for sea trout differ widely in northern European rivers. But the clearer and brighter the water is, the more predominant flyfishing tends to be, while spinning and baitcasting has better chances in relatively dark, murky, deep waterways.

Spinning with spoons, plugs and spinners is done primarily for silvery ascending fish and strongly coloured sea trout. The fish select the same holding places as brown trout, and sea trout are then often caught by spinning downstream. In general, small artificial lures are used in small streams with little fish, while large baits come into play for big fish in wider waters.

Opposite: Sea trout live in the ocean during most of the year, but run up rivers in the autumn to spawn. The seagoing trout seldom weigh more than 4.5-6.5 lbs (2-3 kg), but in some places – notably the Baltic – they can be much heavier.

Vital facts

Sea trout spawn in the autumn, and the fry stay for 1-3 years in the waterway. When 16-22 cm (6-9 in) long, they migrate to the sea during March-April and, the same year or the next, return up the same waterway. Trout that have spawned go to sea in early spring, and some die – mainly males. Once in the ocean, they need a few weeks to regain their condition, becoming shiny and fat. Towards autumn, when ascending the waterway, they acquire spawning colours and the males develop a hooked lower jaw.

The ascent begins early in large waterways, but during autumn in small ones. Unlike salmon, sea trout ascend under cover of darkness – and they usually choose dark, protected resting places, whereas salmon often swim freely in the current. Sea trout do not normally feed in fresh water, and when they do it is not because of hunger. Their willingness to bite is connected with the development of spawning colours, milt and roe. The shinier a fish is, and the less mature in regard to milt or roe, the better its probability of biting in fresh water. Coloured fish do not bite eagerly – except those with strong dark colours, which can become aggressive as the spawning time approaches.

Sea trout ascend waterways in the greatest numbers when the water level is rising or high, so the fishing is usually best then. Newly run, silvery trout still have their bite-instinct from the period in salt water, and take bait regularly in large waterways. In smaller ones, fortune smiles during the evening, night and morning. The biting behaviour of sea trout also varies considerably with their environment. In Great Britain and Norway, fishing at night is common – but in Denmark and Sweden, for example, the fishing is excellent on dark, windy days with a high water level.

A sea trout obeys its instinct to bite for a short time after leaving the ocean and running up in fresh water.
Flood tides and/or high water levels tend to provide the best conditions for hooking this fish.

Frequent choices of bait are spinners weighing 5-12 grams. Their substantial resistance in water makes them well suited to deep, slow retrieval, although fresh-run fish can be gluttonous and relish a spinner or other lure that is retrieved fast. Spoons are used less, but have long been reliable for sea trout in Swedish and Danish waterways. Early in the season, naturally coloured lures in silver/black or yellow/black are popular, but late in the season – when the fish are strongly coloured – fluorescent hues may have greater success.

During the winter, sea trout in the ocean do not tolerate normal salinity and low temperatures. They either move out to warmer deep water, or else migrate into fjords or up the lower parts of rivers. These fish are often small and not yet mature – in Scandinavia they are called "Greenlanders". Their appetite is diminished by the cold water, but otherwise they are in fine condition. Only small bait can catch them, such as spinners, worms or – when spinning – little flies, as mentioned above for brown trout.

In some countries like Denmark, Sweden, Poland and the Baltic states, there is also spring fishing for out-spawned sea trout. It is best in mild weather, but can deteriorate rapidly with the slightest variations in water and air temperature. The condition of spawned-out fish is acceptable in certain waters, yet in others they may be very starved and should be returned.

Sea trout fishing with natural bait

Whether in a Norwegian river, a minor brook in the Hebrides, a Danish or Polish stream, fishing with worms is one of the safest methods for sea trout – from the newly ascended and coloured fish to the Greenlanders and the spawned-out emigrants.

One can fish in small streams with a worm, float, and no weighting. In large waterways, one uses single fixed floats that can carry sinkers of 1 to 10-15 grams, depending on the depth and current. A sinker on the end of the line, and a leader with a worm hook, allow you to make the hook glide in the current before the sinker – a more delicate presentation. A leader with 1-1.5 metres (40-60 inches) to the hook, and a short leader to the sinker, is quite common in rivers with comparatively great depth and good current.

However, worms are not the only type of bait applicable to sea trout. Cooked red shrimp are a superb alternative, especially in the spring and for Greenlanders. During the cold season and in spring, trout or salmon roe is used on single or treble hooks.

A clump of worms, consisting of 3-4 lively earthworms on a single hook, can be extremely effective for sea trout in flowing waters. A bit of red wool yarn on the hook makes the morsel even more irresistible.

When fishing with worms, cast the bait obliquely upstream and let it bounce down along the bottom, while you follow it with the rod and reel in any loose line. The tackle combines a three-way swivel with one leader to the current sinker and one to the hook carrying the clump of worms. The same tackle and technique can be used if you fish with a spinning fly: just replace the hook and worms with, for instance, a tube fly.

Rainbow trout

The rainbow trout (*Salmo gairdneri*) originally inhabited North America, in the mountains north of Mexico up to southwestern Alaska and the Aleutians. It also occurs in Kamchatka. The first examples came to Europe by way of Germany in 1880. Next the species reached Denmark, inspiring many pond farms. As a pond fish it then spread to numerous countries, some of which implanted it in waterways. This has been done on several continents, since the fish is rather robust and tolerates higher temperatures than brown trout do. Today it lives in Africa – for example Kenya, Morocco and South Africa – as well as in Japan, New Zealand, Tasmania, Australia, and in South American countries including Ecuador, Chile, Peru and Argentina.

Hallmarks of the rainbow trout are its purple or pink stripes along the side, and lots of black spots on the back and fins – mainly the tail fin. It has thirty subspecies, but its progenitor is the cutthroat trout (*Salmo clarkii*) which occurs in North America, from Prince William Sound in Alaska down to northern California and several of the Rocky Mountain states. There are also various crosses between rainbow trout and the cutthroat, which itself has at least six subspecies in western America. Moreover, we find cutthroat which are anadromous. Those inland could once weigh nearly 20 kg (44 lbs), although seagoing cutthroat seldom exceed 6-7 kg (13-15 lbs). The cutthroat is not considered as interesting a species for sportfishing as rainbow trout.

The rainbow trout lives stationary in rivers and streams, where it rarely weighs over 2-3 kg (4.4-6.6 lbs). Further, it has a lake-living form that, during most of the year, remains in lakes and only migrates up the tributaries in order to spawn or feed, chiefly eating salmon roe. Perhaps best known are the rainbow trout in Alaska's Lake Iliamna, where they grow to more than 10 kg (22 lbs). The Kamloops trout becomes even bigger.

Anadromous rainbow trout – called steelhead – migrate between rivers and the ocean. In their home waters, the Pacific rivers of the American west and northwest, they approach weights of 20 kg (44 lbs) at some places, although 4-8 kg (8.8-17.6 lbs) is commonest.

Vital facts

Unlike brown and sea trout, the rainbow trout spawns in flowing waters from January until early May. In waters with brown trout, the two species compete intensely. Where rainbow trout have been implanted or have escaped from farms, we often observe normal spawning behaviour – but without reproduction.

The rainbow trout does not seek the same holding places and territories as brown trout. It thrives in current edges and the main current, but in shallower waters, and it is more mobile than brown trout. In many North American rivers with ascending salmon, the stationary rainbow trout pursue the diverse salmon species (such as king, coho and sockeye), living at times on salmon roe. Also in contrast to brown trout, rainbow trout flourish in small groups or schools. They always feed on insects, larvae, leeches, crustaceans and so forth, though not as prone to eat fry and fish as brown trout are.

Appreciated as an implantation fish, the rainbow trout exists in numerous put-and-take waters, where it patrols pelagically along the shores. It often gathers at inflows and can also live in free water, even at fairly great depths.

Above: Compared with other trout, rainbow are more mobile and frequently swim in schools. They are also more attracted to shallow waters, both at current edges and in the main current. Further, they prefer smaller artificial lures with strong colours.

Left: Although rainbow trout usually eat larvae, insects and crustaceans, they can also, of course, be caught with baitfish such as sculpin. Worms, salmon eggs and roe are other natural baits that may appeal to them.

Spinning for rainbow trout

The artificial baits preferred by rainbow trout are small ones, whereas brown trout take both small and large lures. Since rainbow trout stand more freely in the current, the same methods of spinning can be used as for brown trout. This is also true in lakes and put-and-take waters. Rainbow trout have a definite taste for red colours and fluorescent, or bright red or orange, lures – ranging from little red spinners to orange flies for spinning.

Rainbow trout fishing with natural bait

The manner of catching brown trout with natural bait can just as well apply to rainbow trout. It benefits, however, by decorating the worm hook with a bead or a piece of orange or red wool thread. Fishing with salmon eggs or roe is also quite effective for rainbow trout, which eat roe during the winter regardless of whether they live in a western American or a Scandinavian river.

In put-and-take waters, these fish are often caught with diverse types of red or orange dough-balls that contain salmon-egg flavouring. Berkley's Power Bait assortment is the best-known type of dough for them. The balls are fished either stationary with bottom tackle, or with floats. In both cases, the baits become more lively if you retrieve them slowly with long pauses.

Steelhead

The seagoing form of rainbow trout inhabits rivers in western America. Also called steelhead by sportfishermen are the lake-living form in North America and the rainbow trout found in the Great Lakes. But the seagoing steelhead is silvery in the ocean and in lakes, as well as during its run upriver. At first sight, it can be recognized only by the many black spots on its tail fin, adipose fin and dorsal fin. After a short time in flowing water, its characteristic pink stripe becomes clearer. As spawning approaches, the fish grows spotty and acquires a pale purple stripe along the side.

Unlike sea trout and salmon, steelhead feed in fresh water and, moreover, they survive the spawning – in contrast to all species of Pacific salmon. Steelhead weigh 2-6 kg (4.4-13 lbs) but, notably in the rivers of British Columbia, they can reach 15 kg (33 lbs).

The rainbow trout that were brought to Europe have been genetically manipulated to yield the perfect farming fish. Yet some still have their instinct to migrate seaward. Plenty of escaped or implanted rainbow trout in northern Europe thus head for the ocean when they reach a certain size. Marine fish farms of rainbow trout have occasionally even caused accidents, with fish slipping out to wander along the coasts. At many places, they also migrate up waterways, though unable to reproduce.

Spinning for steelhead

In the rivers of western America and those flowing into the Great Lakes, steelhead run during almost the whole year. However, there are distinctive spring, summer and winter runs. As a rule, the fish ascend Pacific rivers all year round too, but with some variations depending on the latitude.

Steelhead are famous in flyfishing literature, especially with reference to small, clear rivers in the states of Washington and Oregon. But they also take different types of spinners, and roe in particular – a trait that is shared by the "steelheads" caught in Scandinavian rivers. Steelhead migrate upriver in small schools, and choose holding places in a manner that recalls salmon. Generally, they select neither dead water nor the fastest water. Current edges and middle furrows in a waterway are ideal stops for steelhead.

Here one can catch them on, for instance, small spinners which are fished across the current or retrieved slowly over the bottom. It is important to fish near the bottom, especially in northern British Columbia; and many western American rivers are fished stationary with so-called Spin-N-Glo. These light spinners are "anchored" with a leader and a lead weight on the bottom, the line is pulled taut, and the rod is placed in a Y-shaped branch. When a steelhead passes the baits or sees them from its holding place, it usually bites. The treble hook on a Spin-N-Glo can also be provided with roe before it is "parked".

Some rivers in Washington and Oregon are fished with small shrimp-like crustaceans, weighted with light sinkers. In other rivers, and around the Great Lakes, fishing with salmon eggs or roe is extremely popular. Using one to three big salmon eggs on a little single hook, perhaps weighted with a couple of lead shot, is an easy and elegant way to catch steelhead. Elsewhere, bigger roe clumps are set on a correspondingly larger single hook.

In Scandinavian rivers and streams, steelhead are often caught as a by-product of fishing for brown trout, sea trout and salmon – on spinners, spoons, plugs and flies alike. Roe, too, is used to catch them in some Danish streams and southern Swedish rivers which are renowned for abundant ascents of rainbow trout.

Opposite top: The steelhead is the seagoing form of rainbow trout. When fresh-run, it may look confusingly like a salmon, but is easy to identify by the numerous black spots on its tail, adipose and dorsal fins.

Opposite bottom: Steelhead are fished near the bottom, ideally with small spinners. These are powerful, pugnacious fish and can cause hair-raising fights if challenged with the right gear.

Arctic char

Besides having a seagoing form, the Arctic char (*Salvelinus alpinus*) lives in cold clear lakes, mountain rivers and brooks with Arctic temperatures. Its distribution, spanning the whole northern hemisphere, includes northern Canada – for instance Baffin Island – as well as Greenland, Iceland, northern Norway, Sweden, Siberia and Alaska.

Furthermore, we find Arctic char in central and southern Norway, southern Sweden, Finland, the Lake District of England and Scotland, mountain lakes in the Alpine countries, and the former Soviet Union. Yet the stocks outside the normal area of distribution often have small fish, as in the Lake District and many Alpine lakes, where even dwarf forms occur. An exception is Lake Sommen in Sweden, which has yielded char of 8-9 kg (18-20 lbs). The fish usually weighs 0.25-3.0 kg (0.55-6.6 lbs), but the seagoing form can grow remarkably large, as on Baffin Island where examples over 12 kg (26 lbs) have been caught.

Arctic char belong to the numerous salmon species that evolved from the same progenitor at the same time – when a land bridge existed between Siberia and Alaska. This bridge caused the evolution of a southerly strain of char – the Dolly Varden (*Salvelinus malma*) – and of a northerly one which spread to Canada, Europe and Siberia. The two species are very similar, and are related to the brook trout, which – along with North American lake trout – is thought to share the same progenitor.

Spinning for char

Char live on small bottom animals, and sometimes on fish fry or larger prey. Precisely because their food comprises so few animal species, they tend to be selective. During the short summer, they may swim in the surface and take insects.

Above right: Landlocked Arctic char are found primarily in areas with an Arctic climate. Typical of the species are its red-orange or red-pink abdomen, and its dark green back with green spots. These colours, already strong, are reinforced when the fish acquires its spawning appearance.

Below right: The seagoing form of Arctic char is shiny when it runs upriver. But after only a short time in fresh water, it becomes strongly coloured in the manner typical of landlocked Arctic char.

Within their region of distribution, Arctic char occur chiefly in lakes, but periodically also in rivers and tributaries. In a lake, the char patrol along the edges toward deep water. With colourful spinners and spoons, one can usually catch them during their hunting raids over the deep edges near land.

Curiosity is a trait of char, and they are easily tempted by artificial baits, but do not bite as eagerly as trout. A trout that follows the lure is immediately frightened if it sees the fisherman, whereas a char seems less timid and often keeps after the bait for several casts in a row. The char in lakes are fished in deep water and above deep edges near land. Both spinners and spoons are fine baits, and should be retrieved in a varied manner upward over the edge, with numerous spin-stops. Small lures with red colours appear to be most attractive.

Vital facts

Arctic char spawn in autumn and early winter. They grow slowly, as do many other Arctic fish. Schools are formed until the char weigh 300-500 grams, and bigger char live alone. Their diet includes insects, crustaceans, mosquito larvae, and snails. The char has a pink or red-orange abdomen, and a dark green back with yellow spots. Its colours become brighter when it spawns. It inhabits lakes, patrolling along the shores, but can also swim in the surface or enter the tributaries and wander up rivers.

The seagoing form, as fry, spends 3-7 years in a river. It emigrates between February and May, to grow briefly in the sea – often for just a few months. Still shiny, it begins to acquire colours after a short time in the river. Males acquire a hooked lower jaw, turning orange-red on the abdomen and green on the back, while females are less colourful. Unlike salmon and sea trout, all char are presumed to run upriver each summer. They eat little during their river journey.

One of the surest ways to make char bite is to replace the treble hook on a spinner or spoon with a short leader of 20-40 cm (8-16 in), to which a trout fly is tied – for example, a simple, classic fly such as Red Tag Palmer or Black Zulu. Spoons and spinners are retrieved slowly with lots of short jerks and spin-stops.

The use of a casting Buldo and a leader with fly is also effective for fishing in lakes when the char hunt insects at the surface. Retrieval must be slow but at an even tempo. Char bite cautiously, and only when their resistance is felt should you strike.

In mountain brooks and rivers, char prefer the calmest areas. The lure is retrieved as in trout fishing. Possible holding places are searched, or the cast is laid obliquely downstream to let the spinner move in the current while you retrieve it.

The American Dolly Varden behaves in exactly the same way as the char, and can be caught by identical methods.

As for seagoing char, their willingness to bite has been found to differ across the Arctic region. In Canada, Greenland, Iceland and Siberia, they gladly take spoons – but in the clear rivers of northern Norway, they quite seldom take spoons or spinners. As mentioned, they eat very little when they run up rivers, and the longer they stay in fresh water the more enthusiastically they take artificial baits.

The fish are inclined to swim in the quieter parts of rivers, where they can hold in limited schools. Small spoons, possibly with a red hackle or red spots, are excellent for seagoing char. Retrieval has to be slow and deep, the spinner ideally going just over the bottom. When you manage to catch one char, others are likely to be at the same place. The fish rise with high water, so the fishing usually depends on the tides and melting snow.

As the fish migrate up through lakes, they grow more interested in biting. Here they patrol the edges toward deep water and frequently swim in the surface. They now increasingly resemble the stationary char in behaviour and way of life.

Char are caught with natural bait as well – for instance worms, larvae and maggots. However, it is primarily in spinning and flyfishing that the species has gained such popularity.

While Arctic char mostly eat insects, spinning with spoons can be rewarding, especially if the treble hook is replaced by a 10-cm (4-inch) leader and a little fly.

Eastern brook trout

The eastern brook trout, (*Salvelinus fontinalis*), has the same progenitor as do North American lake trout and Arctic char. Its natural distribution lies in eastern North America and westward to the Rocky Mountains, but it is readily displaced by rainbow and brown trout. The richest stocks of eastern brook trout are in Labrador, where the Minipi River with its tributaries is best known for one of the largest stocks of fish weighing up to 3 kg (6.6 lbs). Also famous for this species is God's River in Manitoba.

Eastern brook trout were introduced to Europe for pond-farming in the late 1800s, but were out-competed by the rainbow trout. Still, they have always been regarded as one of the most beautiful trout species, and were thus implanted in many of Europe's clear mountain rivers and streams, where they continue to thrive. They rarely become bigger than 30 cm (12 in), while those in ponds can reach 2 kg (4.4 lbs). Today, they are cultivated to some extent and the species is crossed with rainbow trout or ordinary brown trout. It has also been implanted in Argentina.

Spinning for brook trout

All traditional lures are applicable to these fish, with the same methods that catch other trout in brooks, rivers and streams. Big specimens in the northeastern United States, though, are caught on large lures – mainly spinners and spoons. The

Vital facts

Spawning occurs in autumn and winter. The fry grow slowly, living on insects, larvae and crustaceans; once larger, they add young fish to their diet. Eastern brook trout are characteristically found in sizeable rivers with calm currents. In the Minipi and God's River, they also take mice and lemmings. Small stocks of the species have proved to be anadromous, migrating between rivers and the sea, but seldom are as big as the stationary freshwater-living ones, or as pale and shiny.

retrieval should be relatively deep and slow, since the fish does not take food in the surface as often as rainbow and brown trout do.

The fish's lovely colours and deep red, fine-tasting meat have made it a popular implantation fish in many put-and-take waters, whose temperature and clarity suit this much-liked species. Moreover, it can be caught with worms and other natural baits, in the same way as rainbow and brown trout.

The brook trout is a relative of Arctic char and lake trout. This beautiful fish is native only to North America, but has been implanted in Europe and other regions. Large spoons and spinners usually catch it, if fished deeply and slowly. Shown at right is a colourful pair of brook trout while spawning.

From the mid-19th century until some decades into the 20th, many well heeled English fishermen journeyed to Norway in quest of salmon. This painting from the same period still hangs in one of the socalled "English houses" where they lived during their visits.

H·R·H· THE PRINCE OF WALES VISIT TO SYLTEBÖ ERISFJORD AUGUST 1885.
COUGHT IN SEAPOOL BY OFFISERS OF H·M· ROYAL YACHT "ALBERT AND VICTORIA". WEIGHT 35 LBS.

Atlantic salmon

The Atlantic salmon (*Salmo salar*) has given rise to a sport-fishing culture and history that no other species of fish can approach. It existed over a century ago in most European countries, but its stocks have declined due to dams, pollution, intensive professional fishing, and diseases – so much that, in central Europe today, it inhabits only a few rivers of northern Spain and France. Yet it still visits many rivers in Great Britain and Ireland, Iceland and the Faeroes, one river in Greenland, and hundreds of rivers in Norway, Sweden and Finland, as well as in various Russian rivers.

Salmon diseases come primarily from marine farming and, despite repeated efforts to restrict them, it has to be observed that the wild salmon in northern Europe face a risk of extinction in the near future. Probably even the genes of "wild salmon" will be strongly blended with those of cultivated salmon, which has serious implications for the wild salmon's survival, especially in Scandinavia and Scotland.

Atlantic salmon are also found in North America, running up rivers in New Brunswick, Quebec, Maine and Nova Scotia. Only in this region, during recent years, has it been possible to see improvements in the stocks – thanks to the buying up of salmon quotas from professional fishing in the North Atlantic. Perhaps one of the most virgin areas with intact salmon strains is the Kola Peninsula, although the discovery of its world-class fishing in the 1990s has led to a minor decline even there.

The Atlantic salmon is often termed the "king of fish", as it is strong and full of fight, besides reaching weights over 65 lbs (30 kg). Fresh-run individuals are silvery and – unlike sea trout – tend to have only black, cross-shaped spots above their lateral lines.

Vital facts

Atlantic salmon spawn in rivers and streams during autumn and early winter. The fry stay in the waterway for 2-3 years, and the silvery young salmon migrate to the sea during March-April. After 1-2 years at sea, each salmon returns to migrate up the same river, to the spawning bed and the brook where it was born several years earlier. This is one of nature's most astonishing feats, and has fascinated people for centuries.

The salmon ascent takes place from early spring until well into autumn, depending on the latitude. After a time in the river, the salmon become coloured, and males develop a strongly hooked lower jaw. The struggle for females and spawning places is hard for males, and some of them die after spawning – as do some females. How much of the stock perishes, though, we do not know for sure.

The surviving salmon descend to the sea and, at best, come back up the river once or twice in the following years. Compared to other species, the fry have a high survival rate – but things can go wrong, both during the spawning and while the yolk-sac fry are still in the spawning pit. Rain, melting snow and high tides, for example, can destroy the spawning banks or silt them over, so that the fry die. And if the fish do grow up, they occupy territories in competition with, among others, stationary trout. In many waterways, predatory fish such as pike may consume young salmon, especially when they travel toward the sea. Hydroelectric turbines and similar obstacles also reduce the stocks.

Salmon strains develop differently. Some have genes giving faster growth than others. Small salmon, or grilse, together with medium-sized salmon of 4-7 kg (8.8-15.4 lbs), predominate in all rivers, while large salmon of more than 10 kg (22 lbs) are common in few. The best-known rivers for big salmon include the Alta and Namsen in Norway, the Mörrum in Sweden, the Derwent in northwest England and the Tweed on the border between England and Scotland, besides certain rivers in the Kola Peninsula.

Spinning for Atlantic salmon

Salmon fishing involves a paradox: what is the point of serving food to a creature that eats nothing? Ever since the sport began, fishermen have wondered about this, for the fish do happen to bite. There are many theories about why they take bait. Fresh-run, silvery salmon often bite with frenzy at the start of the season. Some of us believe that this is because certain individual "springers" retain their biting instinct. Others think they are driven by a need to fight for resting and holding places in the river, chasing other fish away and, consequently, taking a fisherman's bait.

Later in the summer, the salmon accept small lures in the surface, such as a little spoon or a fly. These are presumed to revive an instinct of youth, when the fish lived on insects in the river. Once the salmon acquire their colours, the time approaches to compete over spawning places. They now become aggressive, and take bait for that reason.

Factors like the weather play, of course, a considerable role. Not the least important is the water level. When it changes, the salmon grow uneasy. Whether it rises or falls, therefore, the fisherman has a good chance – though a falling level is usually best. Both precipitation and melt-water influence the fishing in this way. The lower parts of rivers are also affected to some

Left: When the salmon migrate upriver to spawn, they are in good condition and thus a favourite quarry for sportfishermen. During their swim to the spawning areas, the salmon often have to pass serious obstacles such as wild rapids. River sections with these obstacles are normally good for fishing, since the salmon pause here before resuming their journey.

Right: Several theories exist as to why salmon bite in rivers even though they do not eat anything. Whatever the reason, it remains true that they can be coaxed to take artificial or natural baits. A time-tested method of salmon fishing is to put a piece of red wool yarn and a clump of earthworms onto the hook.

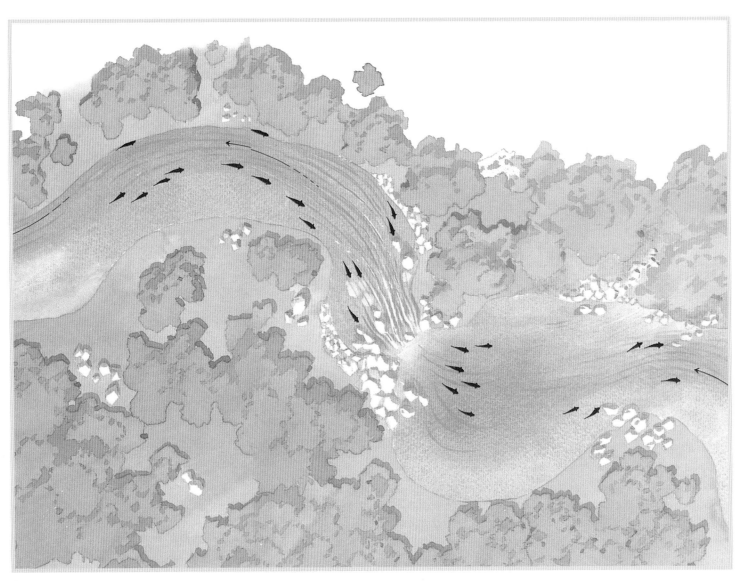

A typical river stretch, shown above, is illustrated below in cross-section. Salmon occur mainly at the inflows and outlets of pools. In relatively long and wide pools, however, the fish prefer to hold at the current's outer edges. Yet in shallow or fast-flowing areas, they take positions in the current lee near large rocks.

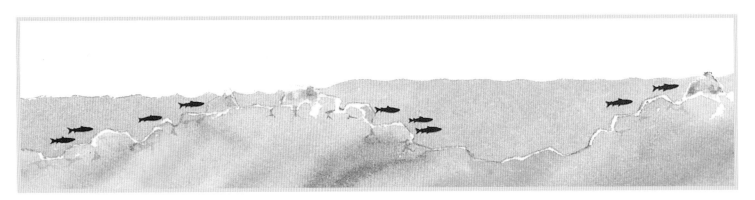

degree by tidal patterns in the sea, as the salmon ascend at high tide and migrate upriver in groups or small schools. Thus, one often finds that the salmon have distinct biting periods in the lower stretches.

The holding places can be very diverse. Large salmon choose the most suitable places, commonly in deep water, while those of medium and small size are banished to shallow water. Salmon often select a current edge, but the necks of rapids are excellent, and long current furrows are ideal.

Some places are more appropriate for flyfishing than for spinning. Yet if, for instance, you see only 2-3 metres of water at the opposite bank – or amid the current – and one metre at your own bank, this is a good site for spinning.

Early in the season, when the water is cold and the level high, you should fish so deeply and slowly in the river that you occasionally feel the spoon or plug hit the bottom. This can be done by casting toward the opposite bank, or obliquely downstream, and then lowering or raising the rod to keep the bait moving at the bottom. As a rule, shiny salmon at a given place will bite during the first two or three casts. To go on casting at the same place any longer is usually a waste of time.

In the middle of the season, the water has sunk and the holding places have changed. One seldom catches salmon in totally calm water, so the bait should move with the current, at the same speed or a bit faster. If the bait slows down, lift the rod or reel in a little line – and vice versa if it moves too fast, although in general it will do better if moving too fast than too slowly.

When the water level is low and the temperature exceeds 10-14° C (50-57° F), the salmon often go into faster water. While their holding places change during the season, so does the size of ascending salmon. The big salmon tend to arrive at the beginning of the season, followed by medium-size and small ones. However, large individuals sporadically run even at the end of the season in many areas. Also late in the season, the fish become coloured and more aggressive, frequently biting after several casts at the same place.

Salmon fishing in a river of average magnitude calls for strong spinning equipment: either a baitcasting reel or a spinning reel, with line of 0.40-0.45 mm, except later in the season when a line of 0.35-0.40 mm can be sufficient. But in small rivers, lighter equipment is used. Spoons, spinners and plugs are excellent bait throughout these months. Early

in the season, spoons of 20-40 grams are often used, as the salmon then stand deep and the water level is high. Many people also fish with floating or sinking plugs of 11-13 cm. Once the water has sunk, spinners of 8-15 grams may be tried too.

Experience shows that, well into the season, salmon take small bait – chiefly flies. Spinning can be done with a fly aided by a casting bubble, or some other kind of casting weight. The flies are of the same type as in flyfishing, such as small single- or double-hooked ones of size 2-10. The leader should be 3.5-4 metres (11.5-13 feet) long, and the fly should swing in the current – as if you were flyfishing. A casting bubble works best in big, lazy rivers, where you can speed up the fly as it swings toward your bank.

Spinning is also possible with a fly and no casting Buldo. Instead you fish with a leader of 1-2 metres (3.3-6.6 feet) to the fly, and a leader of about 20 cm (8 in) to a suitable sinker. This tackle is superb during the whole season, and the fly can be fished exactly like a spoon. Early in the season, and in cold water, one often uses large bushy red-yellow tube flies of 12-16 cm (4.8-6.4 in) with simple patterns. Later on, black or dark tube flies are best. The fly may "hang" in the current, but it becomes more lively if, at the same time, you "pump" it forward and backward in the current – for example by lifting and lowering the rod with some quick movements. Here is an elementary method that can reward the newcomer, too. Yet remember that spinning with a fly is prohibited in, among other countries, Norway.

Fishing for Atlantic salmon with natural bait

Salmon will also take natural bait, though fishing with shrimp is not allowed in Norway. At many rivers in Great Britain, shrimp are still fished on hook tackle. A single hook is used in some places, and one or two small treble hooks elsewhere. Even whole, dead baitfish on hook systems were previously employed in salmon fishing.

Most common, however, is fishing with worms. In certain countries such as Ireland, fishing with a float is widespread, while worms on bottom tackle are used in other lands. The hooks are normally of size 1/0-3/0, baited with a bunch of worms. Attached to the hook are a leader 1-2 metres (3.3-6.6 feet) long, and a second leader that is weighted with a fairly heavy sinker, so that the worms swing in the current at the same speed as a spoon or fly.

Striking, fighting and landing the fish

Salmon bite in many different ways. Some take the bait explosively and hook themselves. Others are more cautious and require you to strike. If fishing with natural bait, both shrimp and worms, you may feel the fish either taking violently, or "chewing" on the bait for several seconds – perhaps up to a minute – before swallowing it, which is the signal for you to strike. Inexperienced salmon fishermen have notable difficulty in judging when to strike, if fishing with worms or shrimp. After the salmon bites, it should initially be allowed to run the show. This is true of all fishing – but in the case of salmon, patience is essential. A further paradox of the sport is how many people react when they hook their first salmon: as soon as it bites, they want to get it up on land immediately, since they are afraid of losing it. Instead, let the fish set the pace, and look for a place to land it only when it shows signs of tiring out, for example by turning its belly upward.

A salmon is landed with a firm grip on the tail. It becomes paralyzed and is quite calm when lifted out of the water. On smooth, shallow shores, the fish is best slid onto land. You walk backward and, every time the salmon thrashes, pull it a little up on land, until it lies on its side and can be lifted high and dry.

Many fishermen also use large nets, although these can be hard to handle. The gaff, too, is still used in some European countries. A tailer is a gentle landing aid, but it demands adeptness. In America and in the Kola Peninsula, there are special restrictions on fishing and rules for returning the fish to water. For instance, in Kola all the fish must be returned.

Powerful rushes may enable the fish to escape from the hook, or to break the line. The closer the fish is to the rod tip, the greater the risk of losing it. By quickly lowering the rod tip, you can prevent a rushing fish from tearing itself free. But the line should always be stretched taut, and the drag should not be set too hard.

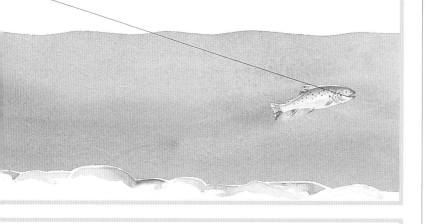

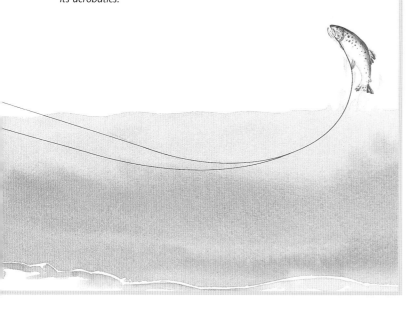

Even when the fish shows an urge to leap out of the water, it is best to lower the rod tip and, if possible, keep the rod parallel with the water surface. This reduces the pressure on the line, and usually makes the fish stop its acrobatics.

In contrast to the majority of other fish species, a salmon can be gripped securely around its tail-fin root. It then becomes immobile, and lets itself be lifted or dragged ashore in a calm manner.

King salmon

The king salmon (*Oncorhynchus tshawytscha*) is the biggest among the six species of Pacific salmon. Five of these live on the American side of the Pacific Ocean, while the sixth – cherry salmon – exists only in Kamchatka and northern Japan. Other names for the king salmon are the chinook, quinnat, spring, and tyee. Specimens of 30 kg (66 lbs) are not uncommon, and whoppers weighing over 40 kg (88 lbs) have been caught in rivers such as the Kenai in Alaska and the Skeena in British Columbia. But the average weight is 8-12 kg (18-26 lbs).

Unlike the other salmon species, king salmon are known for their migrations far up into river systems. In the Yukon River, they swim almost 3,000 kilometres. King salmon in the sea are silvery with irregular black patches, even on the back and tail fin. Moreover, they have black pigment on the mouth and throat. This species is distributed from northern Alaska to California and, on the Asiatic side, from Kamchatka to northern China. It has also been implanted in the Great Lakes, where it thrives and grows to 12-13 kg (26-29 lbs).

Spinning for king salmon

These fish bite much more eagerly than Atlantic salmon do – from the moment they approach the river mouth to the time they begin spawning. Trolling fishermen are busy already in the sea and estuaries, and fish are pursued with artificial baits and salmon roe as they run upriver. For holding places, they choose deep holes, current edges, brinks and backwaters. But unlike Atlantic salmon, they often prefer deep, dark, calm water. Many rivers are murky and partly muddy, so the inflows from clear tributaries can be counted on as holding places – especially at the creeks in which king salmon spawn. Only young king salmon, weighing up to 2-3 kg (4.4-6.6 lbs), rise to the surface for small bait such as flies.

Atlantic salmon usually betray their presence by leaping in the river, but king salmon almost always go to the bottom and

stay there. They often stand in dense schools, whereas the medium-sized and large Atlantic salmon are territorial and gather only at difficult passages or rapids.

During the fight, king salmon are considerably heavier and tougher than Atlantic salmon – yet by no means as wild and ungovernable. Just after biting, they normally show themselves once at the surface, while an Atlantic salmon may leap repeatedly as it struggles.

This fishing needs heavy equipment, often combining line of 0.40-0.60 mm with a very strong rod. Lures for king salmon include the Pixie, Spin-N-Glo, Tee Spoon, and diverse deep-going plugs that ideally contain rattles. Virtually all types of artificial lure work well, if fished deep and slow – almost crawling over the bottom, down to the salmon or

Left: The giant of Pacific salmon is the king (chinook) salmon, which can weigh over 90 lbs (40 kg). Those that run upriver during the spring and early summer are silvery, but the ever later migrants become increasingly coloured.

Above: *Robust equipment is needed to catch king salmon, as they are tough and heavy during the fight. In addition, they gladly choose deep holding places, where the lure has to be fished just over the bottom.*

Vital facts

There are various strains of king salmon. They migrate upriver from January until late autumn, but the primary ascent in most western American rivers is made between May and early July. In contrast to coho salmon, the king salmon runs up large rivers, and it spawns from July until November. The fish that ascend during springtime often choose tributaries, whereas the autumn-running fish select the main river. A further difference is that the salmon ascending in early summer are always silvery, while the late ones are slightly coloured as they ascend. All the salmon die after spawning, as do other salmonoid species in western North America.

The fry feed on insects, crustaceans and larvae in the waterways. They migrate into the ocean during the next or the following summer. Dead salmon fertilize the basically barren waterways, so their fate is naturally beneficial. On reaching the sea, the young salmon grow rapidly, and 2-8 years later they return up the same rivers.

among them. The salmon stand close together and, to avoid hooking them badly, it is only allowed in many rivers to use single hooks.

Nobody questions the power of king salmon – they are tough until the end. Since they usually form schools, one can catch several in the same place. Evidently they are not as shy as Atlantic salmon.

In the Great Lakes, fishing is also done from the shore around river mouths. Between early summer and early autumn, there are chances of catching king salmon when they migrate up the rivers. This is a typical wading sport, and succeeds best in the morning or evening, as the fish swim into deep water to eat during the daytime. One uses strong spinning rods, line of 0.30-0.36 mm, and spoons of 20-40 grams. Piers and breakwaters, as well as sand-banks and headlands near these ascent rivers, are other good fishing sites for king salmon.

Fishing for king salmon with natural bait

As the salmon approach the estuaries, they are subjected to intensive trolling – called mooching. The fish are caught with artificial lures, but whole or half herrings on hook tackle are also popular. When the fish run upriver, it is generally safest to use salmon roe, particularly if all else fails. Salmon roe is often packed in orange nylon net with fine meshes – as big as a walnut – and set on a single hook. Then the roe clump is fished with either a float, free line, or bottom tackle, allowed to swing in the current toward the salmon. In contrast to Atlantic salmon, which frequently bite on one of the first occasions when they are presented with artificial or natural bait, the king salmon is characteristically coaxed into biting by repeated casts with roe.

Left: A king salmon does not leap as often as an Atlantic salmon. During the fight, it shows itself at the surface only on rare occasions – like this!

Right: Once the king salmon have migrated up in spawning rivers, a cluster of salmon roe serves well as bait. A fine-meshed nylon stocking can be used to make clumps of roe. These are placed on a single hook and fished swinging in the current to entice a salmon.

Coho salmon

The coho or silver salmon (*Oncorhynchus kisutch*) is, along with king salmon, the most popular sportfishing species in western North America. It occurs from California to Alaska, besides Kamchatka and down the coast to Japan. It is entirely silvery, with small black patches over the lateral line, back and fins. Its average weight is 3-6 kg (6.6-13.2 lbs), although individuals are known to reach 12-14 kg (26-31 lbs). In 1967 these salmon were successfully implanted in the Great Lakes, where – together with other trout and salmonoid species – it has contributed to the region's impressive fishing. Coho salmon migrate upriver from July until early October.

Spinning for coho

Coho are also caught at sea, as are king salmon. Trolling or mooching for them is very common. They take spoons, or herring on tackle, at river mouths and in nearby marine waters. In the Great Lakes, spinning is done at the estuaries and from adjacent banks, headlands, piers and breakwaters, just as for king salmon.

However, the coho is more eager to bite than king salmon are. It migrates up small coastal rivers, often in sizeable schools, and then chooses quiet stretches of water or current edges as holding places – but it keeps away from other salmon, such as chum. Unlike king salmon, it is content to stay in relatively shallow water. If the river flows through lakes, one frequently finds big schools of coho leaping at the outflows.

Coho are primarily a wonderful quarry for flyfishing, but they can be caught with small spinners of size 2-3, and on spoons of 5-12 grams. While king salmon are readily duped by bright red-orange spoons and spinners, in the case of coho it is better to use spoons and spinners made of silver or brass. Small baits should be retrieved slowly, as close to the bottom as possible – without losing speed. The bite is often cautious but resolute, and only when you start to put pressure on the fish does it begin to leap, approaching the surface much more frequently than a king salmon does.

Almost no fishing with roe is done for the coho, in contrast to king salmon. Thus, it is a distinctive spinning and flyfishing species.

Above: *The greedy coho (silver) salmon normally weighs under 22 lbs (10 kg) and migrates up small rivers near the west coast of North America, ranging from California to Alaska. There it tends to remain in relatively shallow water, and eagerly takes small, colourful spinners and spoons.*

Right: Coho are generally cautious biters, but become lively when they are hooked and feel the line's pressure. Frequently, they leap in the air and thrash in the surface more than they stay in the water.

Vital facts

The coho runs up large rivers as king salmon do, but more commonly it chooses small coastal rivers when migrating into fresh water. In addition, it travels a shorter distance up the rivers than do king salmon, and thus exposes itself less to the dangers and difficulties faced by that species.

Coho are silvery during their run upriver, but later in the season one can also see lightly coloured fish ascending. The spawning takes place between October and February. The fry migrate into the sea either during the next summer, or 1-2 years later. They remain there for 2-4 years, although seldom wandering as far from the home river as do king salmon. In the ocean, coho feed on shrimp, cuttle-fish and fish. The stock of silver salmon in western American waters has decreased in recent years.

Fishing in marine waters

Cod

Throughout winter, English surf-fishermen challenge the cod (*Gadus morhua*) along their country's southern coasts. In Scotland, it is caught all year round. American coastal fishermen vanquish it during autumn and winter, from Cape Cod to Nova Scotia. Much-desired by practitioners of spinning in Norway, Denmark and Sweden, it has not surprisingly given rise to many of the traditions in coastal fishing.

The cod's main distribution covers the North Sea and the coasts of Norway, Iceland and the Faeroes, but it is also common on the east coast of North America. Its colours vary, though: on mixed bottoms in shallow water it is dark brown, while cod from sandy bottoms and deep water are paler. Red, or mountain, cod is the term for cod that live in shallow water and have a strong red-brown to deep orange colour, even on the abdomen.

Coastal cod seldom weigh more than 3-4 kg (6.6-8.8 lbs), except at some places in Norway – such as powerful tidal currents – which regularly yield specimens of 8-10 kg (18-22 lbs). But cod at sea can reach striking weights. In northern Europe, 20 kg (44 lbs) is not unusual and fish exceeding 30 kg (66 lbs) have been caught, for example, at Yellow Reef off northern Jutland, in Öresund and off Lofoten. In North America, boats have brought up cod that reach 40 kg (88 lbs).

Spinning for cod

Cod are caught by spinning from harbours, piers, long shallow shores and rocky coasts. They often prefer deep water and mixed bottoms. The spinning equipment must be robust and long-casting, such as rods of 9-11 feet with strong multiplier or spinning reels, line of 0.30-0.40 mm, and spoons or pirks of 20-40 grams in silver, copper, red or fluorescent colours. Since the cod is a bottom-fish and often goes into seaweed after being hooked, you can benefit by replacing the treble hook with a single hook, which causes much fewer bottom-snags.

One of the most frequent errors, when spinning in deep water, is to start the retrieval immediately after the impact. Spoons or pirks are then retrieved high over the bottom –

In many parts of Europe and North America, cod are caught regularly by coastal spinning. These fish are so widespread in some regions, especially in northern Europe, that traditional coastal fishing is based on them.

without being seen by a single cod. Thus, the lure must be allowed to sink the whole way down, before you tighten up the line and begin to retrieve. The rod is lifted and lowered, as you reel in the spoon or pirk so that it constantly grazes the bottom. In the shallows near land, these movements should continue but the retrieval is a little faster. This technique can be refined once you have a correct feeling for the given depth and bottom conditions: a retrieval that keeps the lure just above the bottom will soon seem natural.

Bottom-snags are almost impossible to avoid, but the worst ones are prevented by choosing the right weight on the spoon or pirk, combined with the right retrieval speed. Unfortunately, cod fishing often means lost lures. If you do not get a bite, the reason may be that no cod are present because the bottom is smooth, sandy or muddy. Cod are

Vital facts

There are many strains of coastal cod, often with different habits of migration and spawning. When the spawning time approaches, they head for certain marine areas with suitable temperature and salinity. Spawning proceeds from January until March and, in some places, also during April. Subsequently, the cod disperse to shallow areas and banks in the sea, or toward the coast, where their diet includes crustaceans, crabs, sand lance and herring.

The cod's senses of smell, sight and feeling are highly developed, and it uses them all when seeking food on the bottom. It can also be found in the middle layer or the surface, hunting sand lance and herring. The best season for coastal cod is from autumn until early spring. Yet at northerly latitudes, as in Norway, the warm months and especially autumn are thought most rewarding.

nearly always found on mixed bottoms with stones, seaweed, mussels and the like.

Dropper flies occasionally give results – due not to simultaneous bites on the pirk and dropper, but since the dropper is better at stimulating cod to take. You can use droppers made of feathers, plastic worms, or single hooks with jig tails. If fishing with a dropper, you must attach strong leaders of, for example, 0.45-0.60 mm line – or even stronger line in areas with big cod.

When the cod hunt herring or sand lance along the shores, rapid retrieval is most effective, as the cod frequently bite a little above the bottom or in the middle layer. At other times, cod are selective and may only swim at the bottom to eat crabs. It is then especially important to spin with good bottom contact, and make the spoon or pirk almost crawl across the bottom to imitate a crab. Under these conditions, red-coloured spoons are superior. Generally, cod in deep water enjoy taking spoons and pirks with bright yellow and red colours.

However, in shallow water and along gentle shores with 2-4 metres of water, varied bottom vegetation, seaweed and stones, it is wrong to use the above technique of retrieval. Strong spinning equipment is still used here, such as a rod of 9-11 feet, line of 0.30-0.40 mm, and a pirk or spoon of 15-30 grams. As soon as the lure hits the water, you start to retrieve at a uniform tempo, possibly with a few spin-stops, so that the lure goes in the middle layer – neither in the surface water nor too near the seaweed.

Regardless of whether you fish in deep or shallow water, there are often more cod where you catch one. The area can be searched with casts in a fan pattern or, along shallow shores and cliffs, by walking for some metres and making parallel casts outward. In such places, the times before and after sunset are good for fishing, as the cod then move toward land.

If you fish from a boat over shallows, it is best to drift across promising current edges or areas known to have cod. This method involves two principal techniques. First, the pirk or spoon can be let down on the side that the boat drifts away from – the wind side – and the rod is continually lifted and lowered, maintaining bottom contact. Second, you can cast with the wind from the lee side and retrieve while jerking the rod up and down. The latter method demands good contact with the spoon or pirk, since you must also compensate for the boat's drift.

Spinning for cod is often done from rough coasts with breakers. The essential equipment includes long rods, strong reels, 0.30-0.40 mm line, and long-shafted nets. Shown at far right is a much quieter form of coastal spinning, from a float-ring close to the shore.

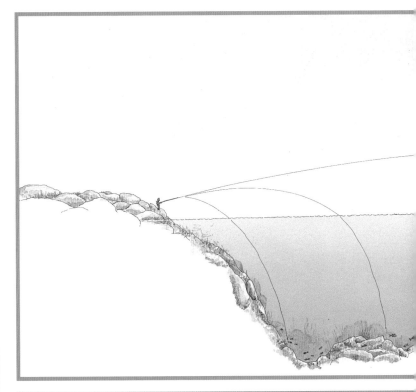

Cod fishing with natural bait

Scandinavians traditionally spin for cod with artificial bait, either from a boat or from land. In other countries such as Germany, Holland and Great Britain, natural baits are used to catch cod.

The given marine or coastal environment dictates the choice of methods and baits. Bottom fishing with natural bait at cliffs, piers and harbours can employ simple equipment. A strong rod of 9-11 feet, line of 0.35-0.45 mm, and a suitable casting weight, as well as paternoster tackle with one or two leaders, and hooks of size 1/0-3/0, are about all the items you need.

Cod are omnivorous, but some types of bait are preferred: lugworms, ragworms, herring strips, mussel meat, shrimps and cephalopods. After baiting and casting the hook, you can either hold the rod in your hand or lay it, within view, on a cliff or place it in a rod-holder. As soon as a cod bites, you make a strike.

At open coasts with sandy beaches, hard current and waves, surfcasting gear is essential. The rods are 11-13 feet long, specially designed for this rough environment. Most people prefer baitcasting reels, but spinning reels work well too. Due to the wear on the line when casting, it is necessary to have an extra-thick line tip, which must be long enough to form 5-6 turns on the reel spool before the cast. The cast itself requires a lot of training and, not least, familiarity with the equipment and how it is loaded.

Fighting the fish

When a cod bites, it heads for the bottom to hide itself among seaweed or stones. A superficially placed treble hook will thus easily catch in the weeds. You must therefore quickly put pressure on the fish, to lift it off the bottom. This is called "pumping in" the cod. With hard lifts of the rod, it is forced upward, while you reel in line each time the rod is lowered. The fish can be landed with a gaff and net, or slid up onto land where this is allowed by the coastline.

Left: Cod often occur where the water is deep even near shore and the bottom is thus not influenced by weather, wind and tides. Here they can hunt close to land, so a relatively short cast is sufficient.

Below: A cod usually weighs 1-5 kg (2-11 lbs). It is seldom a hard fighter, but appeals greatly to gourmets. By quickly "pumping" it up from the bottom after it bites, you can avoid bottom snags.

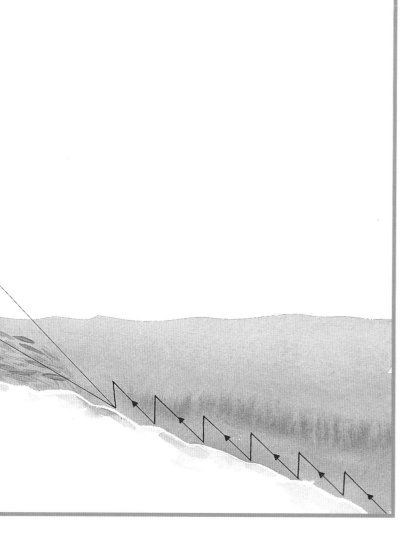

Left: Since the lure must be retrieved just over the bottom, snags may be hard to prevent. But as illustrated here, it is easier to lift the line over seaweed and other vegetation with a long rod than with a short one – especially when the lure approaches the shore.

European pollack

The European pollack (*Pollachius pollachius*) is one of the greatest challenges along rocky coasts of the Northeast Atlantic, where the chances are best of catching this beautiful fish. It is easy to recognize from its bronze-yellow, torpedo-shaped body, big brown hunter's eyes, strong underbite, and notably the dark lateral line that distinguishes it well from the coalfish. Although a type of cod, it has no barbels.

Pollack occur from the Faeroes and northern Norway to Morocco and the Mediterranean, but are chiefly distributed around the British Isles as well as southern and central Norway. They prefer rock coasts with good current and water circulation, living mainly at depths of 4-5 to 50 metres but found as far down as a hundred metres. They are drawn primarily to wrecks, sunken rocks and underwater cliffs. At the coasts, they weigh 0.5-2 kg (1.1-4.4 lbs), and examples up to 4-5 kg (8.8-11 lbs) are seen. Farther out to sea, wrecks have yielded pollack of 9-10 kg (20-22 lbs), which is the maximum.

Right: Pollack are a type of codfish but often live pelagically. They are fast and strong, and large pollack can offer exciting sport with powerful rushes toward the bottom.

Vital facts

Known spawning grounds exist off southern Norway and in the North Sea, where the spawning lasts from February until April. When the young are a few centimetres long, they wander toward the coasts, where they grow up, living on worms, crustaceans and fishfrye. Once larger, they eat small fish – mostly sand lance, herring and sprat – but sometimes also mysis shrimp and other small crustaceans. The pollack is not a bottom-fish like cod, but holds a bit over the bottom. At sundown and on dark, windy days with disturbed water, it usually moves up to the middle layer. It may even be found in the surface at dusk.

Spinning for pollack

Since they tend to hunt somewhat up from the bottom, at rocky cliffs or in surface water, pollack can be caught with relatively light spinning equipment. Exposed rocky coasts with strong currents and deep water are ideal places.

When spinning, it is most important to search all water layers with light, lively spoons or pirks, preferably in subdued colours such as copper, red/copper or green/blue. Pollack are occasionally rather fastidious, and may only take a certain bait of a special colour, size or type. Jigs are often superb for pollack. A little compact pirk with a single hook, carrying a fish strip, is also very lively and inviting.

The retrieval can be made with accelerations ending in long stops. Then the bait sinks through the water and can be reeled in again. It is during the pause, or when the bait resumes moving, that the pollack usually bites. The bite is hesitant and heavy, followed by a violent rush toward the bottom – which means your drag must be finely adjusted.

Droppers are effective, too, particularly in daytime when pollack take small lures. However, the risk is that the leader will snap if the fish dives and the pirk catches in seaweed.

Pollack fishing with natural bait

The pollack is a distinctly predatory species suitable for spinning, but it can very well be caught with natural bait that is fished with a float in breaking waves. A small float with a hook of size 1-1/0, baited with attractive fresh-cut sand lance, herring or mackerel, and swaying irresistibly in the swells, is excellent for pollack. Nor is it uncommon to catch these fish while float-angling for wrasse, which thrive in the same coastal environments.

Top: Jigs can be the right medicine for evasive pollack. Pirks baited with fish strips are also attractive when the pollack are choosy.

Bottom: Pollack are commonly found along rocky coasts where the water is kept moving by, for example, currents. In this case the pirk and droppers have crossed the path of a school of pollack.

Coalfish

The coalfish (*Pollachius virens*), widely called pollack, is another member of the cod family. Characterized by a dark-grey back, white lateral line and shiny tin-coloured abdomen, it lacks barbels and has a clear underbite. Its distribution resembles that of cod, but the southern limit goes through the Bay of Biscay, the northern boundary passing Iceland and southern Greenland. Coalfish also occur along the eastern coast of North America, from Newfoundland to New York.

Small specimens are often encountered off rocky coasts, and in deep water close to land – even just a few metres away. Large coalfish, weighing from 5-6 kg (11-13 lbs) up to the maximum of 25 kg (55 lbs), swim as far down as 400 metres.

Spinning for coalfish

These are extremely greedy creatures. Small coalfish, in particular, bite almost anything that moves. Spoons, pirks and droppers are therefore outstanding lures for them. Since the fish often hold in free water, you have to search it from top to bottom when working from a rocky coast, pier or breakwater, and remember that they may be right in the surface when evening or cloudy weather comes. Their hunting for small fish in the surface is commonly revealed by seagulls.

Vital facts

Coalfish spawn in the open sea, between January and April, at certain places with suitable temperature and salinity. The fry consume plankton but, as soon as this stage is over, the fish approach land. Weighing from a couple of hundred grams up to 1-1.5 kg (2.2-3.3 lbs), they may appear in enormous schools offshore, especially at rocks. The young coalfish feed occasionally on shrimp, otherwise on fish fry – mainly herring and sand lance – while the latter species are eaten by larger coalfish. Throughout their lives, coalfish form schools and seldom stay at the bottom, usually swimming some metres above it and nearly reaching the surface. As with European pollack, they rise at evening and night or in cloudy, windy weather.

The retrieval must be quick and varied. Keep in mind that coalfish, like pollack, may also bite when the spoon or pirk leaves the surface for a new cast. This fishing is not at all difficult, and anybody can land a fine catch of coalfish with no problems after locating them. While good places for pollack tend to be permanent, schools of small coalfish are frequently found by chance.

Large coalfish rarely swim next to land, so examples of 2-3 kg (4.4-6.6 lbs) are regarded as superb along coasts. But one area where big specimens can be caught from the coast is Saltströmmen, at Bodö in northern Norway. Local fishermen have brought up coalfish weighing over 20 kg (44 lbs) in November and December, a time when few people are out with spinning equipment at that latitude. Such prizes are taken with powerful rods, line of 0.60 mm, baitcasting reels and 200-gram pirks.

Above: The coalfish is a beautiful, gluttonous codfish that gladly takes a pirk, spoon or dropper.

Right: At rocky coasts, small coalfish often swim near land, but they may hold almost anywhere between the bottom and the surface. Varied retrieval, preferably with the countdown method, is therefore important in locating a coalfish school.

Mackerel

The mackerel (*Scomber scombrus*) is the ocean's mini-tuna. Its torpedo-like body puts it among the speed demons of the deep. A pelagic predator, a school fish, and a summer guest in the northern part of its distribution – from the top of Norway, past the Faeroes and Iceland, to Newfoundland – it occurs as far south as the Mediterranean and, in America, Cape Hatteras.

The native North Atlantic mackerel lacks a swim-bladder. An almost identical species, the Pacific mackerel (*Scomber japonicus*), lives from Alaska to Baja California, as well as on the Asiatic side of the Pacific and in the Indian Ocean. It resembles the former species, but has a swim-bladder. A third species is the Spanish mackerel (*Scomberomorus maculatus*), which ranges from Chesapeake Bay to Cuba on the American side of the Atlantic, and along the North African coast to the Canary Isles. Mackerel normally weigh up to 1 kg (2.2 lbs) and sometimes over twice as much.

Fakta i korthet

Makrillen övervintrar på 400-600 meters djup i Skagerrak och väster om de brittiska öarna. Makrillen väster om Irland drar sig in mot de irländska, engelska och skotska kusterna, medan makrillen i Nordsjön på våren söker sig in mot Norges kust, in i Skagerrak och Kattegatt. Innan dess har den lekt på djupare vatten och leken sker i det fria vattnet nära kusten.

Makrillbeståndet har drabbats av stora svängningar och under en lång rad år under 1960- och 1970-talen var fisket dåligt. Yrkesfiskarna fann makrillens övervintringsställen i de djupare delarna av Nordsjön och kunde tiodubbla sina fångster – något som makrillbestånden aldrig har hämtat sig efter.

Spinning for mackerel

When the first mackerel head for the coast, between May and early July, they are hungry and tend to attack any moving object – including spoons, pirks and droppers. But later in July, having fed on sand lance and the young of herring and sprat, they become less eager to bite. It is then chiefly in the morning and evening, as they approach land to hunt, that fishing pays off. Their presence is often shown by gulls and other seabirds, which dive at the mackerel hunting small fish in the surface.

Spinning is done from cliffs, piers and breakwaters, where the water is deep and vigorous. Long-casting equipment with line of 0.30 mm, a shiny pirk of 20-50 grams, and a leader tied of 0.35-0.45 mm line, with a couple of little droppers made from feathers – in white, blue and green colours – suits the work perfectly. The water is searched from the bottom to the surface. Mackerel hunt in all water layers, but at dawn and dusk they swim in the uppermost layer and can frequently be seen in the surface.

Mackerel fishing with natural bait

Float-fishing for mackerel can be done wherever the fish exist. However, primarily in the later summer when they bite less greedily, natural baits usually yield results – even at midday as they go deeper.

Since the mackerel prefer to swim at 2-5 metres of depth, this fishing makes use of sliding floats. A float that carries 5-15 grams of lead is suitable, together with a leader having a hook of size 4-8 and a small fresh-cut strip of herring or sand lance. The fishing depth is adjusted by means of a stop-knot or a rubber stopper. For example, you can fish first at 4-5 metres and, if unlucky, try higher up in the water. When the fish bites, you are seldom left in doubt – but on some days the float only shakes a bit, and you have to strike immediately or the monster goes missing.

There are several species of mackerel. This is the North Atlantic variant, which has no swim bladder and can move easily between different depths. To find the depth at which it is hunting, one must often fish all levels according to the countdown method.

Garfish

The garfish (*Belone belone*) lives along the European coasts from the Arctic Circle, past the Faeroes, down to Morocco. It, too, is a summer fish in Scandinavian waters. The Mediterranean and the Black Sea also contain garfish. Yet its main habitats lie around the British Isles. Some closely related species inhabit tropical and subtropical seas.

Spinning for garfish

This is a marvellous sportfish, slender and beautiful, often seen more in the air than in the water when it has been hooked. One rarely meets a predatory fish which occurs so abundantly and is still so hard to catch.

Garfish frequently pursue a spoon or pirk without taking. Such "imitators" are noticed especially in the early part of the season, before their spawning has finished. After spawning, however, the biting begins and the fish can be sought at headlands or banks, from piers or breakwaters, and off coastal rocks, preferably where the current is strong.

These fish are ideal to challenge with light spinning equipment and spoons of 8-25 grams. Elongated, silvery spoons are best. Treble hooks of thin metal have proved to give superior

Fakta i korthet

Näbbgäddan övervintrar söder om Irland och dyker upp vid våra kuster i april eller maj. Först anländer de stora näbbgäddorna, ofta på omkring kilot, och strax efter kommer de mindre fiskarna. Näbbgäddan leker på grunt vatten i tångbälten och ålgräs när solen skiner och vattnet värmts upp. Leken sker under maj och juni, men kan på vissa platser sträcka sig ända till augusti. Tidigt på säsongen går näbbgäddan i stim. Man träffar ofta på mindre stim i grunt vatten, men när leken är överstånden sprider sig fiskarna och återfinns både i ytan och på djupare vatten. Här äter de fiskyngel, räkdjur och spigg. På sensommaren och tidigt på hösten drar sig fisken bort från våra vatten.

results. The garfish's mouth is small and not always easy to hook. Therefore, many of us remove the treble hook and tie it to a short nylon leader. This should not be longer than the spoon, since otherwise the hook may get caught in the main line during the cast.

The retrieval should be even and rapid. Do not be surprised if the fish follows the lure time and again. Once the fish bites, avoid delivering a strike and just tighten up the line well, to fight the fish with a softly set drag.

Catching garfish with natural bait

While the species is quite suitable for spinning, it also falls for natural bait. All you need is a fixed float with 1-1.2 metres of line to a small hook of size 4-8, carrying a small fresh-cut strip of herring or mackerel. Cast out and let the float lie still or drift with the current. The garfish swallow the bait with no trouble, and then you strike.

Left: The garfish is a slender, rapid swimmer with a long, hard "beak". It can be difficult to hook, but fights admirably and often leaps into the air.

Below: Light equipment, sharp treble hooks, and fast retrieval are the three rules of thumb for conquering garfish. They frequently travel in schools and, once found, can yield an abundant catch.

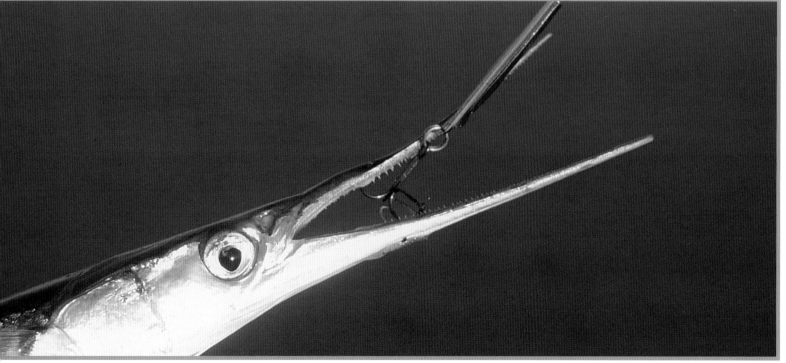

Sea trout

Equally exciting to match wits against are the ocean's silvery racers, sea trout (*Salmo trutta trutta*). Catching them in salt water is a Danish national sport – though also done with flies and Buldos at, for instance, estuaries in Orkney and the Shetlands after World War I. Coastal spinning was started by Danish sportfishermen during the inter-war period, but it developed mainly in the 1950s, at the same time as the equipment became ever better and could cast farther. In recent

Vital facts

Sea trout hunt along all shallow sections of coast that have rivers or waterways which the fish can run up to spawn in. After they spawn and return to the sea, they are emaciated and begin to eat worms, fish fry, herring and sprat. They become shiny and silvery, regaining their weight after a few weeks.

These fish stay along the coasts almost all year round, and can be caught in any month. But some periods are better than others, spring and autumn being excellent. During autumn, though, sea trout are not as willing to bite as in the spring.

The fish prefer mixed, varied bottoms with current, weeds, sand, stone and mussels. Consequently, good fishing places include banks, headlands and rocky points. From May throughout summer, the coastal water in many areas is too warm, so the sea trout move into deeper water, returning to the coast from evening until morning.

Some sea trout migrate up in streams and rivers as soon as June, while others head for fresh water during the autumn and early winter. The winter also brings many shiny non-spawning fish into coves and estuaries with lower salinity – and here they are found on soft, rather uninteresting bottoms.

decades, coastal fishing for sea trout has spread to Sweden, Norway and Germany.

Sea trout are distributed from northernmost Norway to the Dutch and French coasts, as well as around the British Isles. This fishing, however, is popular especially along the coasts of Denmark, southern Norway, and Sweden. The Baltic Sea contains notably large sea trout, and big ones also occur at the Danish coasts. Fish of 2-5 kg (4.4-11 lbs) are not uncommon. On the other hand, sea trout in Norway, Great Britain and Ireland are relatively small.

Spinning for sea trout

Since most sea trout cruise along the coasts, the fishing depends on chance. Thus, knowing what places they visit is very helpful. At the beginning of the year, they are attracted by ragworms, which gather to mate during early spring. Mussel banks and eel grass contain many kinds of animals – such as shrimp, worms, small fish and fry – that draw in sea trout, too. The more open, stony, current-combed coasts, where sand lance and small herring live, can be similarly rewarding.

Limited areas for coastal fishing are searched by casting in a fan-shaped pattern, or in various directions. The open coasts are fished with a cast every five or ten metres, according to the water's clarity.

Fishing is commonly combined with wading, which allows you to reach deeper water and cover larger areas, besides keeping closer contact with the fish itself.

The fishing can be divided into light, and somewhat heavier, spinning. In the former case, one uses spoons of 5-15 grams with light spinning or baitcasting rods and 0.15-0.23 mm line. Elsewhere, one may be forced to fight against wind and weather, requiring longer casts – so one frequently chooses stronger rods, 0.25-0.30 mm line, and elongated spoons or coastal wobblers of 15-30 grams.

Retrieval, during the spring and autumn, should be fast with repeated jerks or spin-stops, at each and every cast. In the winter, since the water is cold and the fish are less active, a calmer and slower – but still varied – retrieval is most effective. Dropper flies can also give results in certain places.

Coastal fishing for the seagoing form of trout requires equipment that is long-casting but relatively light. Good local knowledge, and lures which imitate the fish's natural prey, may be essential during the periods when sea trout are hard to trick.

It is often necessary to cover a promising stretch of coast thoroughly. Finding sea trout may also require one to move along the shore, while making a series of parallel casts or casting in a fan-shaped pattern.

Fishing with a casting bubble and flies enjoys wide popularity. The Buldo is a great aid especially in winter and early spring, when cold water prevails or when the fish are mostly focusing on a single type of food, such as ragworms. It is also worth using a casting bubble in summer until August-September, when sea trout are less eager to bite.

Fishing for sea trout with natural bait

Natural baits are often served to sea trout. Most simply, where the water is deep enough and a stony shore exists, you can fish with a fixed float and a short line to a hook with worms. But the absolutely best method is spinning with a Buldo and a leader of 1.5-3 metres with a single hook and worms.

The baits employed are earthworms, ragworms and herring strips. In some areas, small fish such as sprat and sand lance are preferred. Spinning with a casting bubble and natural baits is done all year round, with a slow retrieval and ideally some pauses so that the bait and hook can sink. If you want them to go deeper, the leader may be lengthened and weighted with a couple of lead shot, or a short piece of sinking fly-line can be tied to the line tip.

Slender spoons weighing 10-20 grams, and a dropper on a short leader of 20–30 cm (8-12 inches), are a combination that not even big sea trout are likely to resist.

Coastal spinning for sea trout should be done by presenting the lure just above the bottom. The retrieval must be varied and lively, with regular jerks and spin-stops, in order to entice sea trout.

European bass

The European bass (*Dicentrarchus labrax*) is the star species of sportfishing in Great Britain. Hardly any other fish around the British Isles has meant so much for the development of coastal fishing, surfcasting, and their equipment. Rods, reels, lines, leaders and other accessories have undergone enormous refinement in recent decades due to the fish's popularity.

These bass live chiefly around the British Isles, in the Bay of Biscay, on the Atlantic coast of the Iberian peninsula, off Morocco and in parts of the Mediterranean. They also occur

Vital facts

Open, surf-filled shorelines are the primary habit of European bass. Along beaches interrupted by rocky outcrops and breakwaters, they hunt sand lance, herring and crabs. Often they wander about at only half a metre of depth. Being attracted to river mouths and fresh water, they can also be caught from piers and barriers that give them shade on bright days in clear water.

Both on coasts with surf and in estuaries, the first hours after an ebb tide are considered good for catching bass. But no other firm rules exist for the fishing. They move to deep water in wintertime, and can be harvested almost all year round in Ireland. The spawning lasts from March until June in the British Isles, and takes place during late winter in the Mediterranean. These fish are widely prized by professional fishermen, and are universally regarded as fine food.

Fishing for European bass can be highly diverse. In some periods it is incredibly easy to get them to bite – on simple bottom tackle, a spoon or a mackerel tackle. At other times, particularly in clear water, they may become extremely shy and suspicious of any bait. Occasionally they fight like crazy, even in water just a few inches deep, or else become very lazy and virtually swim up on land by themselves without pressure from the rod.

in the Black Sea, and some are found at the coasts of southern Norway and western Sweden. The latter region has lately received ever more bass.

Weights of 5 kg (11 lbs) are seldom exceeded, and 1-2 kg (2.2-4.4 lbs) is most common. Professional fisherman, though, have landed bass weighing more than 10 kg (22 lbs). The species belongs to a family with several hundred representatives in subtropical and tropical waters.

Spinning for bass

This fish is caught mainly with natural bait. Despite being a genuine predator with well-developed eyesight, it does not attract direct efforts at spinning in most places. Such spinning is practiced, however, along the Dutch coast at many wrecks in relatively shallow water – with good results on pirks and spoons. In Great Britain, the species' homeland, spinning for it is not so common. To make it bite, the fisherman needs clear water, and thus has little success under murky conditions. The best season for spinning is from June until October. Classic spoons and pirks such as the Toby are excellent for bass. Bridge pillars, piers and breakwaters should be fished from, besides rocky headlands and underwater shoals in shallow water.

Fishing for bass with natural bait

When natural bait is used, these fish can be tempted at all sorts of places – river mouths and fjords, shore structures, open beaches and stony coasts. The fishing is easiest where the cast length does not matter much, as in estuary areas and from piers. Often, though, an acquaintance with the tides is essential, because bass are known for hunting over large shallow areas when the tide comes in. As mentioned, one does well to fish soon after the low tide.

Standard equipment for bass on open coasts is a rod 10.5-11.5 feet long, with a casting weight of 50-90 grams and line of 0.30-0.35 mm on a baitcasting or spinning reel. A thick line tip is also necessary. Bass are usually fished with a paternoster tackle – either fixed, which is most simple and effective, or sliding – and a single hook of size 1/0-3/0. Since the fish-

European bass are extremely popular in, for example, Great Britain – where they have strongly influenced the development of coastal fishing techniques and equipment. Normally they weigh 1-2 kg (2.2-4.4 lbs), but individuals over 5 kg (11 lbs) have been caught.

A number of bass have been landed at last. This voracious predator tends to prefer relatively shallow waters, taking both artificial and natural baits.

ing often occurs amid currents or waves, most people use a breakaway weight that is anchored on the bottom. The baits include lugworm, sand leeches, cuttlefish, sand lance, or small peeler crabs.

The great majority of bass fishermen need only be able to cast 40-90 metres. This is quite enough, as in many places one can wade into the surf – wearing waders. Moderate surf is best, and so is cloudy weather in general, although the fishing can be superb even in strong sunshine. A bite from a bass may show itself in various ways – ranging from a couple of tugs on the rod tip, to a slack line or a ferocious pull on the line.

Left: Breakers and rocky coasts are favourite spots for the coastal fishermen who go after bass. The first hours after the ebb tide are usually most rewarding.

Right: Bass are temperamental fish – sometimes very easy to catch, but shy and wary during other periods. Here, a slender spoon has given good results.

Striped bass

The striped bass (*Roccus saxatilis*) is a favourite of sport-fishermen along the eastern coast of America, from St. Lawrence Bay down to northern Florida, and in the Gulf of Mexico from western Florida to Louisiana. Yet the most famous stretch is from South Carolina to Massachusetts. This fish was introduced on the Pacific coast towards the end of the last century, and is thus also found from the Columbia River mouth in Washington to the Los Angeles area in California. Here the best-known place is San Francisco Bay, whose fishing is far better than on the east coast.

Striped bass resemble the European bass in many ways, but can grow much bigger. Examples approaching 50 kg (110 lbs) have been caught by professional fisherman, and up to 30 kg (66 lbs) by coastal fishermen. The commonest weights, how-

Vital facts

During the eastern winter, striped bass stay in Chesapeake and Delaware Bays. From there, a minor emigration of bass occurs in the winter. The fish spawn in river mouths from April until June, depending on the latitude. One renowned spawning area is the Roanoke River in North Carolina. They weigh scarcely half a kilogram (1 lb) when two years old, and 10 kg (22 lbs) when aged seven. The females grow bigger than the males. Striped bass are more or less omnivorous: their diet includes grey mullet, flatfish, herring, anchovy, lobster, crabs, shrimp and mussels. In spite of that, they eat selectively – when offered a certain type of food, they often concentrate on it and may therefore be unwilling to bite. Some bass stocks migrate locally, and there are two long major migrations every year: northward in springtime along the coasts of New Jersey, New York and New England, then southward in autumn. These occasions, especially the latter, provide the best coastal catches.

ever, are 3-8 kg (6.6-18 kg). On the east coast, striped bass have been fished hard by professionals for long periods, suffering serious stock reduction. Still, this spectacular fish is available if you are on the coast at the right time and place. Moreover, it has been implanted successfully in large lakes in North and South Carolina.

Fishing for striped bass

Spinning is done with very strong spinning or surfcasting gear, and large plugs or spoons. Rods of 10-11 feet, and ample spinning or multiplier reels filled with 0.35-0.45 mm line, are standard. Wind, weather, currents, migrations and, not least, the supply of preyfish are influential – and suddenly these bass may appear for a short time near land, where they can be caught. Early morning and the evening are profitable, but night fishing with natural bait is also common.

Bottom fishing with natural bait is as frequent as spinning. Among the baits used are small fish, worms, crabs, fish fillet, and sand lance. But the leaders, hooks, and other equipment must be adapted to the widely varying conditions of this fishing, from the surf on open coasts to the rocks and breakwaters where spinning is possible. It is tough work, and can prove demanding indeed.

Striped bass may be up to 2 metres (6.6 feet) long, and then weigh about 50 kg (110 lbs), but specimens of 3-8 kg (6.5-18 lbs) are most common. These are distinctive predators and call for comparatively strong gear, combined with either artificial or natural baits. In the tough fishing along wave-worn coasts, surfcasting is the usual method.

Top left: *When fishing for red drum in the "Texas style", one wades out with a big lure until chest-deep. Then the lure is let down and one wades back to shore, to await the fish's bite.*

Bottom left: *Red drum are often fished in the dark hours. These fish live in shallow water – eating smaller fish, mussels and crabs, for instance – and thus take both natural and artificial baits.*

Above: *Tarpon are characterized by their many silvery scales and their bone-hard mouths. They are also, of course, famous for high leaps in the air and for being able to snap the strongest lines...*

Other large sportfish

There are many other fine species of sportfish, such as the **Bluefish** (Pomatomus saltatrix) which is found in nearly all subtropical parts of the Atlantic, in the Black Sea and Mediterranean, and along the Atlantic coasts of the Iberian peninsula, northwest Africa, the Canary Islands, Azores and America. It is hard to give any general advice about choice of equipment since, for example, catching bluefish that weigh a kilogram in a Florida bay is very different from casting against wind and waves on the open coast of New Jersey. Yet under all conditions, this is a fast and wild opponent.

Weakfish (Cynoscion regalis) occur along the east coast of the United States, and can be encountered in the shallower waters of coves and river mouths. This popular sportfish is often easily caught with bottom tackle.

Red drum (Sciaenops ocellatus) are found on the American coast. A bottom fish, living chiefly on crustaceans, this species is best caught in the morning and evening with robust equipment.

Tarpon (Megalops atlanticus) live throughout the Caribbean and along the coasts of many West African countries. A tarpon weighs from a few kilograms up to hundreds, and has excellent fighting qualities. The fishing is normally done from a boat with plugs or natural baits.

Index